GEORGE CLARKE'S
more
amazing
spaces

GEORGE CLARKE'S
more
amazing
spaces

George Clarke with Jane Field-Lewis

Quadrille
PUBLISHING

Special photography by Ben Anders and Richard Maxted

CONTENTS

INTRODUCTION

I absolutely love working on this show. Now into its fourth series, *George Clarke's Amazing Spaces* celebrates the small-scale builds that have been created with big ideas as well as, in many cases, a pretty big dose of courage on the part of the owners.

These relatively small spaces and quirky builds sidestep the processes of traditional architecture but more than make up for this in their imaginative design, the sheer hard work that goes into their creation and the fact that they're real projects designed by individuals to make their lives better. They illustrate the human spirit at its best.

In fact, it's the contributors who made this book and what it's all about. It's their projects that we feature, and in the following pages we can ponder over them in more detail than in the TV show. Many of the builds have an illustrated floor plan to help you see how the space works in its entirety, along with the background story and more information about the build process.

The results of these enterprising owners' endeavours are a pleasure to share. Some of them, such as the modern pre-fabricated, super-cool Hivehaus, are the nucleus of growing businesses, while others, like the Cream-Tea Camper, are set to provide their owners with a new lifestyle and occupation; and then there are amazing builds, like the fantastic Warren, where a young couple has created the ultimate back garden play-space for their children. The potential of the finished projects is huge, and I can guarantee that all the contributors feel wiser and more knowledgeable and have a huge sense of pride and satisfaction. Not all the builds went entirely smoothly and to plan, of course, but they were entered into with a sense of adventure and an

acknowledgement that new skills needed to be learnt and hurdles overcome. Many of the owners have little or no building experience, yet they embraced learning along the way and seeking advice from friends or researching best practices online. I am so grateful that it's not only the good experiences but also the bad moments and setbacks that they are willing to share with us. I find that an inspiration. And seeing these projects develop from the germ of an idea to a successful finish is a privilege.

I'm quietly happy in my professional capacity as an architect, looking out for people without my training or experience, but this is not a series where I'm just a spectator – I'm a contributor, too. My own project presented a unique challenge for me and my team: to design and build something of practical use while pushing ourselves to be creative with everyday materials and off-the-shelf parts. This process illustrates the benefits of clever design, of thinking afresh and trying our best to find new solutions to problems. I'm grateful to have been given that opportunity, and whether it's my caravan (in my previous book) or the fantastic treehouse that opens up to the sky (p104 of this book), or the garden studio/snug/butterfly tunnel (p66), each has been an utter pleasure and an exciting journey, and I look back at each of these projects with great affection.

Finally, I'd like to thank the team who work with me on the series – they're a very special bunch of people. Jane, my co-author, stylist and the creative consultant behind the show, never disappoints with her head full of ideas and total fearlessness when it comes to hard work; master craftsman William Hardie's team are of a similar ilk; and the production units at Plum Pictures and Channel 4 each play their part in the success of the individual projects and the show as a whole.

This level of commitment and ethos are echoed throughout the show – the collegiate effort and willingness to think outside the box rather than sitting quietly at home accepting life and taking the line of least resistance. Even with the humblest of means and budgets, there's still a world of opportunity out there if you have vision, determination and a sense of adventure. I hope you enjoy the real-life stories and images on the following pages. Every one is an inspiration to me and I believe you'll think so, too.

George Clarke

TEXAS ROAD TRIP

TEXAS IS A STATE RENOWNED FOR BIG STUFF, SO THIS ROAD TRIP WAS A FANTASTIC OPPORTUNITY TO GO LOOK AT THE LITTLE STUFF: THE CREATIVE INDIVIDUAL PROJECTS AND IDIOSYNCRATIC HOMES CREATED FROM JUNK, SOIL, JUST ABOUT ANYTHING... WHEREVER YOU GO IN THE WORLD, THERE ARE ENTERPRISING AND TRULY IMAGINATIVE PEOPLE WHO CAN TAKE AN UNASSUMING CUBBYHOLE AND TURN IT INTO THE UNEXPECTED. TEXAS, WHERE EVERYTHING IS LARGER THAN LIFE, IS NO EXCEPTION. WILLIAM JOINED ME ON THIS ROAD TRIP OF A LIFETIME AS WE SET OUT TO EXPLORE SOME AMAZING SMALL SPACES.

CATHEDRAL OF JUNK

Nestled in an ordinary suburban backstreet in Austin, between the "normal" homes, is a weird and wonderful psychedelic structure built entirely out of junk! Vince Hannemann, the owner, is a laid-back sort of guy and has put a huge amount of time (25 years!) and effort into creating this amazing building. As he cheerfully says, "Before it got its name and a life of its own, I didn't know what was going on. I was just playing and having fun."

However, he now has a plan as well as a building permit (he had to obtain one in 2010 when it crossed the line from being "yard art" to a building), and although it's mad, it is beautiful and it's not totally aimless. There's a form and a structure because everything is tied to everything else, as in a bird's nest, so it gets ever stronger. There are even colour-coordinated and schemed areas inside. If you look closely, there's a primary structure similar to a skeleton onto which the junk is fixed, like a sculptural piece.

As you enter, it feels like somewhere you could explore; you follow a winding pathway and emerge into a big, cathedral-like, conical space, and from there you can explore in different directions. Everything leads to the back and the stairs up to a mezzanine level and viewing platform.

Inside it's peaceful and quiet, like the crypt of a cathedral. Vince has used everything in his quest to recycle "trash" into a construction with a life of its own. Look closely and you see CDs, lawnmower wheels, car bumpers, computers, toys, biscuit tins, cables, bottle tops, ducting from an air-conditioning unit, circuit boards and tyres filled with cement in the crow's nest at the very top. You name it, Vince has used it. It took expertise and techniques to put everything together, and it's still evolving as people donate more junk or send it through the mail! This is a remarkable piece of architecture.

ROBOT RANCH

Near Ferris, on the outskirts of Dallas, is the unbelievably cool Robot Ranch. Its concrete arched dome structures were built to merge into their natural surroundings, and it's a marriage made in heaven. It feels almost futuristic, in a post-apocalyptic way. Engineer Al Schwarz is the creator of this extraordinary man-made hill. Using an ingenious technique, he gutted the existing hill and rebuilt it, using a custom-made inflatable balloon-like structure. When fully blown, the interiors were sprayed with insulating foam to make it really rigid. Steel reinforcements and a concrete layer on top made the structure strong enough to be covered with soil and rocks, returning the hill to nature.

It's taken Al nine-and-a-half long years to get this far, and during that time he's moved 320 tons of rocks all by himself. When we visited, he reckoned there were another six months and 50 tons of rocks to go before the big Grand Opening party! What he's created is a unique underground home with 385m² (4,144ft²) of sculptural floor space spread over two storeys and with three interconnected domes. Looking at it now, the building is literally the landscape – the way it terraces up, the two are indistinguishable.

The living area is a vast, open-plan space but, despite this, the utility bills are very low – less than half those of a normal-sized house, and when Al installs the solar panels he will be even more self-sufficient. One of the highlights of the ranch for Will and me was the sunken theatre with a massive cinema screen, bar and pool table – perfect for a boys' night in. There's even a fountain inside!

BEER CAN HOUSE

In Houston is probably the most unusual build I've ever seen. It's a normal suburban house but with one important difference – it's clad entirely in hammered beer cans with their ring pulls hanging down. The idea was conceived back in 1968 by an ordinary man with an extraordinary pastime – retired upholsterer John Milkovisch's hobby was collecting beer cans but, unlike most collectors, he decided to put his collection to good use. It took him many years to drink over 50,000 cans of beer, with a little bit of help along the way from his wife, Mary, but he persevered and the Beer Can House gradually evolved. The result is brilliant.

His disdain for painting his timber-framed house inspired a pioneering idea – to clad it with beer cans instead. Armed with a "can-do" attitude, some scissors, a beater and a hammer, John spent hours cutting and flattening every can before lovingly adding it to the slowly expanding aluminium skin surrounding his home.

It's probably the most enjoyable recycling project ever undertaken anywhere in the world. Will says: "The flattened and cut-out beer cans have oxidised and taken on a wonderful patina. This bloke drank every one of those beers. We'll never look at our recycling boxes in the same way again!" It gives the motto "Keep America beautiful – please recycle", written on every can lid, a whole new meaning.

When the wind blows through the cans, it's like a musical house. As well as being decorative, the cans also act as an insulating outer layer, effectively lowering John's energy bills.

FUTURO HOUSE

A few miles out of Dallas, we had to pull over – we couldn't believe our eyes. Just by the side of the road, as if it had been dumped there, stood an abandoned Futuro house like a UFO that had just landed from another planet – *War of the Worlds* stuff. Covered with graffiti, this landmark is incongruous but super-cool.

Designed by Finnish architect Matti Suuronen, fewer than 100 of these self-contained ski chalets were made in the 1960s, and fewer than 50 remain today. They're still an iconic design. They consist of 16 pre-fabricated plastic pieces that could be assembled in advance or bolted together on site, creating 25m² (260ft²) of space-age-looking living space.

Although it had been vandalised and covered with graffiti, it was still a fantastic space inside, with loads of headroom and great acoustics. It's amazing to think that lots of people didn't like these houses when they first appeared. What a fantastic piece of design – I wanted to pick it up and take it home! It could be such a wonderful project.

LOCOMOTIVE TRAILER RANCH

Away from cityscapes and suburbia, overlooking the banks of the Nueces River in south Texas, this converted, vintage one-bed trailer is an incredible sight. It's uncannily spacious inside, even though it's only the size of a large caravan. A concrete tower was built to anchor the all-steel open deck and to provide space for utilities, a bathroom on the lower level and a viewing deck on the upper level with a vista of the whole ranch. The trailer sits off the ground to protect it from heavy rains and flooding, supported and cradled within a steel frame, while a large overhanging roof covers the 18.5m² (200ft²) sleeping loft and provides shelter from the elements. The decking, which has a hot tub, extends 9m (30ft) out over the river bed.

Inside, the trailer has been restored to its former glory. The uniform bamboo lining the walls, floor and ceiling enhances the sense of space. It's a great example of 1940s' and '50s style, from the finish and aluminium trim in the kitchen to the original and very evocative Spartan Aircraft Company Oklahoma badge on the front of the trailer.

Outside, the 7m (23ft) long, cantilevered balcony is a real piece of structural trickery, winding around the trailer with no supports. I love this mix of the old and precious with the new wrapping around it – it blends seamlessly into the landscape.

EARTH HOUSE

This is a weird and wonderful hand-built structure in an Austin suburban street of conventional timber-framed houses. Earth House is a family home created by DIY enthusiast Thea Bryant for herself and her four children.

This extraordinary construction uses centuries-old techniques in a modern location. It is constructed of adobe mud, cob (without straw) and 30 per cent locally found clay, 220 tons of which were needed. Thea found the whole process very empowering and she got more proficient in time. She had a limited budget and the costs were very reasonable and affordable – $15,000 for the materials plus 4,000 hours of labour, many of which were carried out by Thea and friends.

The house resembles a coil pot of the type made by potters. The 60m² (650ft²) structure has three levels, eight domes and 56cm (22in) thick walls. Inside, every part of it feels hand-made, and it's surprisingly spacious and light thanks to 20 openings for doors and windows. It's a marvellous home.

ETHAN AND KELSEY'S TINY HOUSE

Ethan Ramirez and his girlfriend, Kelsey Bernard, both students and small-space pioneers, live the good life on a peaceful organic farm, surrounded by trees and fields in Tiny Town. Their home in this blissful existence occupies a mere 100-sq-ft white box on wheels.

Ethan explains: "I realised one day that there was a lot to clean! So I decided to shrink my space down to the things I want to focus on and I love." He got inspired when he saw someone buying a tiny house online. He decided that he would make his own version, and although he had failed wood shop at school, he went out and bought a book on woodworking and a few months – and $7,000 – later the Tiny House was a reality.

Surprisingly, inside it is not claustrophobic at all. The high ceiling makes all the difference and there's a huge bed plus storage space and shelving when you climb up the skinny ladder to the mezzanine level. Every spare inch of space is used: there's a hard-working kitchen area including a fridge, a cupboard for hanging clothes, and a desk. Under the loft/mezzanine level are 5 x 15cm (2 x 6in) black beams (not the usual 5 x 10cm [2 x 4in]), and these make an amazing difference in terms of storage. Those extra 5cm (2 in) define where you can keep your cups and other small essential household items.

This feels remarkably like a normal apartment with a rustic, log-cabin feel. And everything is made from off-the-shelf products from a hardware store. I couldn't think of anything that Ethan and Kelsey were missing, apart from a lavatory and shower, but they've got that covered. There's a toilet outside in the "bath house", and when they want to shower they go to their local gym. In fact, the gym membership is cheaper than an average annual water bill!

TEXAS TINY HOUSES

Although Darby is the creator of all these tiny houses, the one pictured left is his pride and joy. This is his own home and it has been lovingly pieced together with treasures from all over the world.

In San Marcos, 50 miles out of Austin, is an extraordinary sight – what looks like a graveyard for every piece of old scrap imaginable. Nothing here is going to waste and, for me, it's paradise. Every last fixture and rusty old fitting is being resurrected to make unique small homes and dwellings. This extraordinary development of small-space projects built from salvaged materials is the brainchild of Darby Lettick. People donate old, broken-down timber houses and he recycles the best bits and pieces and recreates them as really special tiny houses. His collection of scrap has come not only from all over America but the other side of the world as well.

The jewel in Darby's crown is the house he's built for himself – 21m² (230ft²) of footprint, nearly 7m (23ft) long, incorporating over 800 different materials from 30 houses, and a whole year in the making. There are pieces from Buffalo, New York, Minneapolis, Chicago and St Louis, and the coloured glass in the windows came all the way from India. It's packed with history, texture, character and beauty. I love all the different timbers and colours and how the materials are left to reveal their true nature.

What you don't see is the series of amazing subterranean chambers below the tiny house. 1.5m (5ft) down is a camper van, which is accessed through a trap door. And go down another 10.5m (35ft) into the ground and there's a 12m (40ft) shipping container connected via tunnels! And Darby has tunnelled even deeper to create a 7.5m (25ft) pit for storing water, so it won't evaporate in the hot Texan sun. Delightfully eccentric, he even has plans to grow plants for food down there, using artificial light.

Darby's tiny houses and the underground home are extraordinary and, what's more, virtually free, except for all the human energy involved. We all have scrapyards near where we live and we could follow his example and do this ourselves with a bit of creativity.

"[It's a] totally awesome experience. Living here is really minimalistic and changes your view of life. You only have the things you really love around you. If you haven't used something for two months then you don't need it!" KELSEY

HOME SPACES

THE HIVEHAUS

WHEN BARRY BOUGHT HIS CURRENT HOME, HIS PLAN, AS ALWAYS, WAS TO RENOVATE AND DEVELOP IT, BUT THIS ONE WAS DIFFERENT AS IT HAD A SMALL PLOT OF LAND, AND THIS OPENED UP NEW POSSIBILITIES. HIS FIRST BUILDING PROJECT WAS THE OUTBUILDINGS, SOME DISUSED CRUMBLING STABLES. HE TOOK A SLEDGEHAMMER TO THEM, KNOCKING THEM DOWN, AND BUILT A WOODEN CHALET IN THEIR PLACE. HE BEGAN THINKING SERIOUSLY ABOUT SMALL-SCALE DESIGN AND ABOUT HALFWAY THROUGH THE PROJECT HE HAD HIS EUREKA MOMENT – THE IDEA FOR A SMALL-SPACE LIVING CAPSULE RATHER THAN JUST A SMALL-SPACE GARDEN STUDIO. THE PHYSICAL AREA AVAILABLE TO HIM OPENED HIS MIND AND PROVIDED JUST THE CREATIVE OPPORTUNITY HE NEEDED. IT HAD BEEN A LONG TIME COMING.

IN AND OUT
Barry has designed this pod to have one entire wall that is hinged and opens out onto a deck. The neat, simple and contemporary wood-burning stove swings outside, too, creating an eye-catching indoor/outdoor space. How about that!

THE HIVE PATTERN
Bees and the way they use hexagon-shaped wax cells to construct honeycombs had always fascinated Barry, but this shape occurs throughout nature, from flies' eyes to rock formations, and it has geometric and practical qualities. It was this ingenious natural phenomenon that informed Barry's modular design.

DEVELOPING THE IDEA

Over the years, Barry has repeatedly moved and renovated his houses, improving each one along the way. In all his homes he built himself a "man shed" – he loved what these small spaces gave him and designed them to function as a studio as well as a workshop. They were somewhere to keep his drum kit, work on his computer-art projects and generally create things.

The Hivehaus started in the same way as many of the others, with a rough pencil sketch. To take it to the next stage, he put his fledgling idea into his Illustrator design program. Now he could see the Hivehaus as a 2D plan, which was good but not good enough, so he taught himself how to use SketchUp in order to produce 3D drawings to a professional standard.

He also understood the necessity of making a 3D example of his idea, and out of some paper and cardboard he produced some models of his hive pods. He photographed them outside in a natural location for a more realistic image. Being able to see a 3D form makes a huge difference when it comes to grasping the form of the space and, in this case, how the pods related to each other. As Barry says: "It's a great way to visualise what you're trying to do; it's fine to draw it but you can't see round every angle."

THE GEOMETRY OF THE IDEA

In brief, Barry's concept was a modular design. Each module was the size of a small room; and while he discovered lots of people who were making modular buildings using squares, he thought a hexagon was a more suitable shape to grow from and add on to. In essence, by cutting off the corners of a square, the space feels larger and less hemmed in. It's also an easier shape to furnish as there's less pressure to put the furniture into corners, making the whole space usable, more open and fluid.

THE CREATOR

Barry Jackson is one of those fortunate people who, along with great practical skills, has the kind of mind that is alive with ideas all the time. Barry was introduced to building by his father and it became his profession, but outside of work he has always enjoyed expressing himself creatively; he plays the drums, has been in bands, produced their album artwork, taken photographs, learnt Photoshop, written articles and even a book as well as designing the interior of a friend's restaurant. Until the Hivehaus, he had had to channel this creativity through hobbies outside of his day job.

LESSONS LEARNT

Barry was determined to make the pods so that other people could buy and configure them as their own dwellings. Therefore, certain qualities had to be sought. The pods had to be replicable and of a consistent standard; the materials chosen had to be commercially available off the shelf. The walls are pre-cut to allow wiring to be fitted at the client's request. Keeping logistics and delivery under control, each pod had to be able to be delivered in a Luton-sized van. Everything is designed to be flat-packed, easy to assemble and use, and eco-friendly, too.

Each hexagonal pod is made up of six equilateral triangles joined together with their points meeting in the centre. Barry cut out some cardboard hexagons, half-hexagons, diamond shapes and single triangles. Through his modelling he discovered that when adding additional pods, all these shapes fitted together perfectly, so he wasn't restricted to adding only complete hexagons. This created the potential for a greater selection of additional pods – and therefore more flexible room sizes.

MODELLING AND PROTOTYPING

Barry, along with many other creative homeowners, loves watching all the programmes on TV about building your dream property. Because of his enthusiasm for small-space, affordable projects, *Amazing Spaces* was a particular favourite and he contacted the show to generate some interest. It was a way of maintaining his focus and ensuring he followed his idea through to its logical conclusion. To his delight, the producers liked the idea and agreed to include his build in the series.

However, just as things were going from strength to strength, nature intervened, and while he was doing the day job Barry fell off a roof when a ladder he was standing on snapped. His badly broken leg put him in a cast for three months and off work for four months. The filming dates for the show were fixed and there

was no time to be wasted, so Barry used his period of incapacity to refine his sketches and models to a point where he could progress the project towards a business concept and present the concept in a professional way.

LEGALITIES

As with any burgeoning business idea, it's wise to seek advice on how to protect it. Barry knew he needed to safeguard the concept and looked on the internet and contacted local business development organisations about legal protection for his intellectual property (IP). Help was plentiful and he was not only able to obtain IP advice but also to apply for – and obtain – online a start-up loan and business mentoring. He knew that he had to protect his idea, and although being featured on *Amazing Spaces* would be helpful, it was not sufficient on its own, so through his local contacts and intensive research he obtained the design rights and a trademark on the name "Hivehaus".

STRIVING FOR ELEGANT SIMPLICITY

Working on the development of the conjoined hexagonal pod shapes, Barry applied the Bauhaus principle not only as inspiration for the name of the project but also, and more meaningfully, in his construction approach. Form must follow function, and the build was design-led by practicalities. The key decision was when Barry hit upon the framework, which bolts together with vertical poles at each corner of the hexagon – and these poles became the conduits for the drainage.

THE DOME
An off-the-shelf product, the dome is made of polycarbonate and can be double- or triple-skinned; triple is stipulated by building regulations if you want to live in your Hivehaus.

The big open walls came next – along with the question of how to let in maximum light in the easiest way. Each wall is divided into three equal sections. The window section can be one-third, or two-thirds, and there are two sizes of windows available. Similarly, the wall sections were available in two sizes and you could choose whichever combination of wall and glass you liked.

The construction of, say, a timber-framed house, has varying layers of structure, insulation, battens, cladding, plasterboarding and waterproofing. However, Barry wanted something much simpler that was internally and externally finished in one go.

CONSTRUCTION AND MATERIALS
Barry did considerable research to find the materials best suited to his project. For the walls he chose SIPs (Structural Insulated Panels), which consist of an insulated core sandwiched between two structural facings with layers of rock panel (made from compressed basalt rock) – waterproof, non-warping and low maintenance. The middle layer is 125mm (5in) of polystyrene insulating material, and the internal facing layer is Rigidur H. Made from recycled paper and gypsum, it is waterproof, fire retardant and comes pre-finished; no plastering is required.

Made by a company in Yorkshire, these panels are bespoke for the Hivehaus. Each one was deliberately designed to be light enough for two people to carry. Barry was adamant that the Hivehaus must be a quality and comfortable build that utilised the most modern building products available to him.

The walls are supported by everyday scaffolding poles. These sit on concrete pads and are adjustable to keep everything level.

The fibreglass roof is made in three sections, each of which has a drainage point where the water drains down one of the supporting scaffolding poles. This gives the Hivehaus its own internal drainage system and means there are no unsightly gutters or drainpipes. The roof is strong enough to support and hold a "green roof system", such as sedum, so the ground you lose when you locate your Hivehaus can be replaced on the roof.

INTERNAL FINISH

Barry has coined the term "future retro" for his own brand of a modern look inspired by key retro shapes, materials and furniture, along with the space-inspired TV shows of the 1970s. He describes it as "the feel of looking back at the future". For instance, the dining table in the kitchen was inspired by the shapes used in the stylised "Futuro" spaceship-looking homes of the 1960s (see p12). Similarly, the colour palette throughout and the wood finish in the kitchen echo the upholstery fabric and wood structure of the vintage Ercol sofa in the sitting room.

PLANS FOR THE FUTURE

Barry didn't stop at one Hivehaus, and plans are afoot to extend the range. He has set up a manufacturing unit and is starting to take orders for more. On his website he has even developed a 3D design tool that allows potential clients to design their own version and to get a quote immediately. It's a great concept.

THE KITCHEN
The amazingly neat, compact but highly functional kitchen, with its mix of sprayed MDF and solid oak, was designed in collaboration with Barry's kitchen-designer friend, Mick Culshaw. Incredibly stylish, it folds neatly away to look like a cupboard. The doors are articulated and open back to sit snugly against the Hivehaus walls.

BORDEAUX GARAGE

WHEN OUR WORK OR TRAVELS GIVE US THE
OPPORTUNITY TO SEE FANTASTIC BUILDING PROJECTS,
IT'S EASY TO ADMIRE THEM BUT NOT NECESSARILY TO
RECOGNISE THAT THEY COULD BE RELEVANT TO OUR
LIVES, TOO. MANY ARE JUDGED TOO LARGE, TOO GRAND
AND TOO UNACHIEVABLE, BUT IT DOESN'T HAVE TO BE
LIKE THAT. FOR FRENCH PHOTOGRAPHER JÉRÉMIE, THE
AMAZING BUILDINGS HE WAS PHOTOGRAPHING FOR A
FIRM OF ARCHITECTS STARTED A TRAIN OF THOUGHT. HE
DIDN'T DISCOUNT THE RELEVANCE OF THESE BEAUTIFUL
PROJECTS TO HIS OWN SITUATION AND REALISED THAT
IT WOULD BE POSSIBLE TO DO SOMETHING EQUALLY
INTERESTING ON A SMALL BUDGET.

THE REQUIREMENTS

Jérémie's budget of 170,000 euros had to cover architects' fees,
construction work and a form of traditional space like a house.
He thought it would be interesting to start with a blank canvas
and transform it very personally to reflect his needs and tastes.

One day, he spotted an old, empty garage that was in his price
range. "It was just an empty storage space, not even used for a
car. When I showed the photos to my family and friends, they
said 'Ooh la la!' It was quite scary and risky. There wasn't even a
water connection, and the closest was 25m (27yd) away." In spite
of all this, Jérémie wasn't deterred: the location was good, at the
end of a cul-de-sac that used to be an old mews in a desirable
part of town, and although it was very central, it was a quiet, leafy
backwater where the local children could play outside safely in
the street. All in all, it was an extremely pleasant place to live.

PLANNING

First, there were planning requirements that had to be met.
The building is grade-listed by the *Bâtiments de France*, so the
roof and framework of the building could not be changed. The
façade had to be made of wood or stone because the building is
in a protected *impasse* (passage), so sliding doors were fashioned
out of pine to comply with this regulation. In addition, when
you apply for a building permit in Bordeaux, there's a rule that
states you have to create a car-parking space; otherwise a tax
of 15,000 euros becomes payable to the city council as a kind
of fine. Officially, the patio in front of the garage has the same
dimensions as the minimum legal requirements for a parking
space, so this complies with the regulations, but Jérémie doesn't
actually park his car there!

THE CREATOR
Jérémie Buchholtz was born
and raised in Bordeaux
and he had long found
it difficult to locate an
affordable place to live and
work. There have always
been artists and architects
in his family and as he puts
it, "Ever since I was little,
they showed me the hidden
side, the story behind the
building. I always thought
that one day I'd love to build
a beautiful house."

INTRODUCING LIGHT

When Jérémie acquired the garage it was being used as a junk room for storage and there was no light at all. His priority was to create effective ways for daylight to fill the building and he started by making a hole in the roof. Big glass sliding patio doors were installed at the front with the regulation wooden sliding doors in front of them.

THE DESIGN

This was the first time that Jérémie had undertaken such a project, so he commissioned the architectural skills of Julie Fabre and Matthieu de Marien from the firm for whom he takes photographs. With such a limited space, he needed to make it work as a whole, and for this to happen it had to be thought out and designed in an intelligent way. The central storage unit in the shape of a cube is the key piece of furniture and construction. The idea was to keep a maximum of space for the *éspace de vivre* (living space) and to concentrate everything else into this piece of furniture, which would be used to store everything.

But this cube was far more than just a clever storage solution. Jérémie thought long and hard about what it needed to achieve: "It was kind of like a game to think of everything according to my needs. There's a sofa bed for guests (my bed is on top of the cube), a small bathroom with a toilet, a *douche italienne* (floor-based shower), a washing machine and boiler. It has a wardrobe for my clothes, and cupboards for my photography equipment and materials, files and paperwork. There's also an office space for my desk and computer and a hi-fi stereo, and they are all linked not only to each other but also to my photography equipment. Because all the wires and cables are in the walls, the floor is just one varnished cement surface, so the effect is very minimalist, pure and refined." What's more, it only takes five

MAXIMUM SPACE

It was a canny move by the architects not to use all the width and height of the room and to keep such a beautiful volume of uncluttered space. Most people would have built a big mezzanine floor at the back, but the storage unit doesn't take up the whole width of the room and it creates a feeling of airy expansiveness.

LESSONS LEARNT

Jérémie had several friends who had bought places of their own and were doing them up themselves. Some of them made big mistakes and had to start all over again! Jérémie had no wish to follow their example. He had worked alongside the professionals on a variety of projects and admired their skilful approach. It was a rational decision to use their services and then to photograph the build and make some money out of it! The architects supervised everything and made sure that the artisan builders and craftsmen worked to the agreed timescale.

minutes to convert the desk into a dining table if friends come round for dinner.

For Jérémie, this unique space is a *port d'attaché* (home port) where he can chill out and relax. He travels extensively for his work as a photographer and has to be mobile and always ready to lock up and go. The garage is practical because he can open up the house or close it down in five minutes. And now that he owns his own place, he's more at peace with himself.

SLEEPING AREA

As well as a main double bed on top of the cube structure, there is also a sofa bed below for guests.

BASEMENT CASINO

THIS AMAZING PROJECT INVOLVED THE TRANSFORMATION OF AN ORDINARY BASEMENT INTO A HIGH-SPEC, HIGH-TECH PERSONAL CASINO, WINE CELLAR AND GYM/SPA/UTILITY ROOM. AND WHAT MAKES IT EVEN MORE INCREDIBLE IS THAT THE OWNERS DIDN'T EVEN KNOW THAT THIS EXTRA SPACE EXISTED BENEATH THEIR VERY FEET. THE POTENTIAL FOR THIS PROJECT, ARRIVING IN SUCH AN UNEXPECTED WAY, WAS TOO GOOD TO MISS.

THE CREATORS

Mark Brown is a garage owner and car mechanic by trade. He'd followed his father into the family business repairing high-end cars. He studied product design, engineering and innovation at university and helped his father with renovating student houses when his studies allowed. He had always had good practical skills and a natural curiosity about the structure of things and how they worked, loving nothing better than taking them apart and fixing them. His father always encouraged him to "have a go" and "to think things through". This experience ran deep for Mark and stood him in good stead for this difficult and super-skilled project.

PRACTICALITIES

Mark and his girlfriend, Claire, had recently moved into this 1964 four-bedroom, detached house, and as part of making it into a comfortable home they wanted to install some surround-sound speaker wires neatly under the floorboards. When Mark asked the previous owner how he could access this space, the answer was informative and intriguing – there was a hatch but he would need a ladder to access the space. What he discovered was a huge basement cavity that followed the entire footprint of the house, providing an additional basement measuring 36m² (387ft²). They decided to put their honeymoon savings towards the project.

The newly discovered basement space wasn't immediately habitable. The headroom was limited, the slab concrete floor uneven, and there was no daylight there. To remedy all this and to turn it into a dry and bright, usable space was going to take money, time and skill. The building and engineering techniques necessary are usually the domain of specialised construction companies with experience in the equipment, materials and technical knowledge needed for basement excavations.

"I got giddy with the idea of adding a new level to the house. I've always improved houses and sold them on to make money. I've done lots of DIY, knocked walls down, put in lintels, so this was me pushing myself. I wanted to make a cool guy room, a man cave – somewhere I can hold my poker nights with my mates. However, it's gone from being very much mine to very much ours, and we spend a lot of time down there. We use the gym/spa every day before work, and the wine cellar most evenings."

"On a relatively modest budget, what you have done here is breath-taking … the standard and the quality are amazing. You are never going to come back to ground level!"
GEORGE

THE SECRET DOOR

Rather than have a regular entrance door into the basement, Mark felt that adding a bit of mystery and drama would be more fun. The doorway from the ground floor looks like a built-in floor-to-ceiling shelving unit. By turning one of the ornaments fixed to the shelves (a miniature Easter Island head) by 90 degrees, the door swings open, upwards from the bottom. It uses car-boot closing struts normally used for preventing the boot from falling shut. The first pair of struts were too powerful and when they were opened simply punched through the door itself. Mark downgraded the power of the struts (these ones were used on a Peugeot 205) and he also over-engineered the door so there was no way it could break again!

"Sometimes I can't find Mark, so I go looking for him and he's in the cellar just standing in it – then he sees me and says, 'Look what we have done.'" CLAIRE

Mark decided that he and his friends had the combined skills and resourcefulness to dig out the space, install tanking and a sump to keep it dry, install a proper staircase for easy access and add a section of thick engineered glass in the ceiling/floor above to allow daylight into the space. When that long construction list was finished, the basement would become a casino/man cave, wine cellar and combined utility/gym/chill-out space.

THE DIG AND THE STRUCTURE

The basement was only partially in existence, and in order to create enough headroom in the space, the uneven concrete slab floor needed to be removed and the floor level dug down. Mark took it to the lowest level and dug it all out to that point.

The digging and removal of the concrete and soil was inevitably the hardest, dirtiest, heaviest and most soul-destroying part of the job. For Mark, this meant literally digging out 60 tons of earth, which all had to be moved upstairs and taken out of the house. With the help of family and friends, it was accomplished over the Christmas week. They are no lightweight characters; even on Christmas Day they had a human conveyor belt going out of the front door to move the earth. Mark's mate "Lee the liability" is a landscape gardener – "He's a machine with a spade" – and he helped from Day One of this project. Mark recognises that he would have given up without everyone's help; he couldn't have done it by himself – it wouldn't have been physically possible.

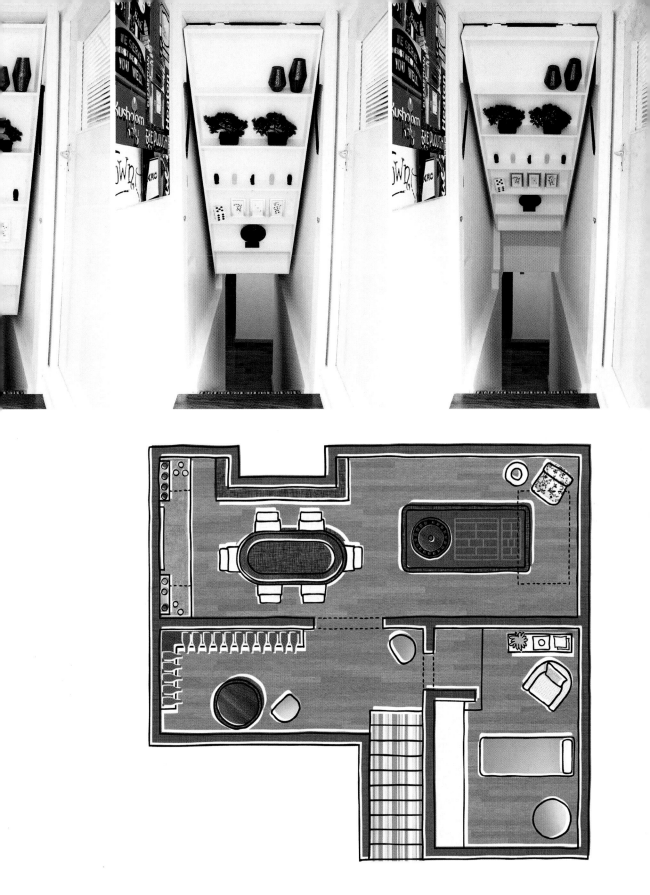

MINI VEGAS

The main room downstairs has been turned into a multi-functional casino/games room with a pool table that can be transformed into a roulette table, a separate poker/card game table, plus a cocktail bar that fills the length of one wall with built-in beer chillers beneath.

THE GLASS FLOOR

Finding a means of getting natural light into an enclosed basement area is a challenge to most basement projects. Adding a panel of structural glass and letting in natural daylight from above hugely improves the feel of this basement space. Mark knew that the basement was something of a dark hole and he had seen George using this concept in his TV series *Restoration Man*. The 25mm (1in) engineered glass makes the space feel bigger and brighter and outweighs the loss of secrecy that Mark was looking forward to.

Most of the structural work had already been done in so far as the house had been built with exceptionally deep foundations, and even with the dig the foundations of the walls and rafts of concrete underneath the chimney breast were carefully left in place. It would have been a big job to take it out, and there would have been a huge structural and cost issue in doing so.

Mark took advice from a structural engineer with regard to maintaining the structural integrity of the building. He realised early on that certain areas of the basement could not be dug out, and although this reduced the amount of usable space available, it was preferable to the serious structural supports and excavation that would have been necessary otherwise.

KEEPING THE WATER OUT

In any basement, groundwater is ever present and desperately trying to find its way into the property. To prevent this ingress, the basement walls had to be lined with a waterproof membrane (a heavy-gauge specialist material) that allows the water to run into drainage channels dug around the edge of the floor. These drain into a sump, which pumps the water out constantly. This is serious work and it has to be carried out successfully or the area will flood. Mark knew that he was taking on a staggering amount of risk here and sought specialist advice. The task needs to be done well, and it's imperative that the sump pump is utterly reliable and up to the job. The complete honeymoon budget just about went on this one crucial piece of kit. It is a dual pump, with one standing by to step in should the other one fail, and there's a battery back-up in case of a power cut. This is a serious business.

THE FINISH

The whole of the basement area has a very high-quality finish; Mark wanted no tell-tale signs of the DIY nature of the project.

The wine cellar was made of oak, with LED strip lighting highlighting the wine-storage area. Even the old barrel used as a table with two sleek organic-shaped metal bar stools has been beautifully finished. Mark had it soda-blasted to remove the dirt and grime from the exterior without stripping it as harshly as sand-blasting would have done. The space feels grand.

The casino/games room bar area has glass shelving fixed to a graphite grey polished plaster wall. It has a lustre and a glamour more often seen in the cocktail bars of five-star hotels.

The materials are all sleek and highly finished. But Mark was determined that the upmarket atmosphere of the space shouldn't be a case of surface dressing alone, and the materials used and the way they have been worked and applied emphasise this fact. Mark and Claire had researched the decorative details of various casinos in Las Vegas, collected their ideas and then tied them all together in a contemporary style.

KEEPING NOTES
When Mark first embarked on this project, he got a notebook and made lists of the envisaged stages of work, the potential complications, the advice he would need to seek, and much more. By this process, he always felt in control of the project and had a clear plan of what was ahead.

He started by looking at the basement space and asking himself some key questions: Is a conversion even possible; how will it be built, how will we keep it dry? He knew he would have to enlist the services of a structural engineer to advise him on what could and couldn't be done, and he made a note to speak to friends Dave, Ed and Chris about the rendering, structure and tanking, respectively.

Other questions he noted down concerned the type of footings and foundations he would need and how far he could dig down. He made several structural and layout sketches, too, and kept updating his notes and drawings when he came across new discoveries.

THE WINE CELLAR

The smallest space in the basement is an oak-lined and shelved wine cellar where the couple can relax at the end of the day. A fridge is installed to keep everything at the correct temperature, and a small seating area created for the two of them to sit and enjoy a chat and a glass of something nicely chilled.

THE SPA

The medium-sized space within the basement is multi-functional. For daily use it houses the washing machine and tumble drier, as well as home gym equipment. An area was also created as a more tranquil chill-out zone and spa. It is a functional, quiet space.

MISSION ACCOMPLISHED

The sense of space that has been created in this basement is fantastic. A neglected subterranean dark, damp area has been transformed for a relatively small amount of money. Digging the basement out, after checking that the structural integrity of the house would remain intact, provided the headroom required to make it usable, even allowing for the loss of space by adding flooring and plasterboard. It was a joint project between not only the two of them (Claire designed and painted it, and Mark built it) but all the friends and family who pitched in and contributed, too. I don't think that it could have worked any other way.

For Mark, it is "...a real feeling of achievement. Seeing people's reaction to the space is great. My aunts and uncles came round the other week and their reaction to it was great – they were so impressed. It's given me a huge amount of personal satisfaction."

This couple had set themselves a budget and stuck to it, and now they are setting their next target and saving furiously for that honeymoon. It took four months of extremely hard work, but they have created the most gorgeous space and extended their house in such a way that it will be easy to use it for relaxing, having friends round, having a laugh and just enjoying life.

LESSONS LEARNT

When digging revealed that four crucial walls were sitting on the current slab floor, the vital question "Should we continue?" was posed. They realised this would be a structural compromise and that there couldn't be a DIY solution.

Mark thought it through; after conceding that he couldn't risk it, that the drainage plan was ruined, and after wondering if it was worth continuing, he carefully re-drew the plan of the possible basement, colouring in red the areas that could not be excavated or removed. And he continued to ask himself whether it was worth continuing with this compromise.

If the area was reduced, there would less area to finish, more budget for the main room, no need for fewer games, and just a smarter use of space required.

THE LUXURY
NARROWBOAT

BUYING A RUN-DOWN PROPERTY CAN BE A DAUNTING
PROSPECT FOR THE UNINITIATED, OR THOSE OF US
WITHOUT THE NECESSARY SOURCES OF KNOWLEDGE
OR SUPPORT. BUT BROTHERS MATT AND ROB WENT ONE
STEP FURTHER AND BOUGHT A BURNT-OUT AND RUSTY
BOAT. MOREOVER, THOUGH THERE WAS ENTHUSIASM,
THERE WERE NO BUILDING OR DIY EXPERTS IN THEIR
NETWORK OF FAMILY AND FRIENDS, SO THE CHALLENGE
WAS FOR THEM TO COMPLETE.

THE BOAT

The boat they found was 18m (58ft) long by 2m (6ft 6 in) wide and was in a pretty frightening condition. Badly damaged in a fire, which had been extinguished, it had sunk to the bottom of the canal before being craned out, its ballast removed and then transported by road to a boat repair yard. The back section was entirely burnt out and it was a mess, but despite this the boat was relatively young (built in 2007), the hull was good and it had a good head height. It had potential even though there was a lot of work to do in rebuilding it.

Like many of us contemplating a big spend, the boys were apprehensive and they spent two weeks deliberating about the purchase. They weighed up the pros and cons and considered from every conceivable angle whether it was a good idea. Their final decision to go for it was made one evening in the pub, although they cheerfully admit that it was based more on gut instinct than as a result of reasoned thought.

When they took possession of the rusty and flooded wreck their only salvation was that the purchase price included some of the essential restoration work. The engine would be serviced, the exterior, steelwork and some of the portholes repaired, a work floor installed and the boat painted. That was substantial progress but there was considerably more that had to be achieved in order to make the boat into anything vaguely habitable or even desirable.

THE DESIGN

One of the key challenges when designing the interior of a narrowboat is the obvious one: by definition the boat is extremely narrow in relation to its length. These boats were designed for a life on the canals and first built during the Industrial Revolution, but they are blessed with good light from windows along both sides, and they open up at each end and often in the middle, too.

The boys wanted to create a modern, open-plan living space and avoid dividing it into smaller rooms linked by a corridor. This would maximise the light and space available inside the boat. Only the bathroom would be a separate room. The boat was to be a communal, homely space where family members and friends could gather, so the main living area had to feel spacious but still include enough seating to make everyone feel comfortable and relaxed.

THE CREATORS

Brothers Matt and Rob Carter had thought about buying a boat together on and off for years. They lived at home but wanted to invest in something and have a place where they could stay and hang out with their friends, or rent out when they weren't using it. Their vision was to buy a run-down canal boat, fix it up for Rob to live on throughout the winter months from October to April (but still go home to Mum's for Sunday lunch!) and rent it out during the summer.

Rob and Matt have an architect friend who kindly did some scale drawings for them; this helped them to work their way through various ideas – on napkins and scraps of paper – for the interior layout.

THE WORK

Neither Matt nor Rob possessed any carpentry skills or DIY knowledge whatsoever and they had to learn fast. They asked lots of questions, looked information up online and their friends came to help. The main job for the boys was fixing the interior plywood to the wooden battening; and as Matt says, "We didn't really know what we were doing." They borrowed tools and bravely had a go, learning that different thicknesses of plywood were required for different tasks – 18mm (¾in) for strength in the lower panels, 9mm(⅜in) in the upper panels, and a thinner 6mm (¼in) ply in the ceiling to bend it around the curve of the roof.

The ballast ("a great big pile of bricks") that was used to keep the boat at the right height in the water had to be reinstated and this task was physically very hard. Painting the exterior was less demanding, but first they had to decide on a colour, which was more of a collegiate decision. Rob wanted teal whereas Matt favoured orange; in the end they decided to go with both and to

avoid the traditional decorative paintwork seen on many canal boats. Theirs was going to be a modern, sleek version rather than a conventional folk-inspired boat.

The windows were all replaced with new ones – squarer windows at the front and portholes at the back – all of which were bought from the manufacturer of the original windows. However, they couldn't do everything themselves and there were some jobs that required professional expertise. They commissioned electricians to install the electrics and the rooftop solar panels that charge up the batteries in the back of the boat.

The bathroom is accessed via a small set of wooden steps leading down from the back of the boat, while a cleverly conceived curved wall increases the sense of space and avoids any awkward corners. The other bathroom wall functions as the rear wall of the bed area.

THE SLEEPING AREA
Over time the bedroom morphed from being a separate space with folding doors into a simple bedroom alcove with a futon that could also serve as additional daytime seating.

BACHELOR PAD
Turning a boat into a home is always going to produce a characterful result, but this one additionally bears the characteristics of its young owners, from the musical touches to the beer barrel fitted with a working pump.

At the front end of the boat a simple kitchen and breakfast bar were installed, with a shallow metal trough sink on the opposite wall. And, as a finishing touch, a wood-burning stove was placed on a slate hearth to heat the boat and make it cosy in the winter.

LEARNING ON THE JOB

Narrowboats are going through a period of change and are witnessing a re-invention. The traditional decorative boats with numerous dark, small internal spaces are being adapted by the younger generation, who are looking to create affordable and individual living spaces. Matt and Rob have created something very special here. It's a move away from home for them and a place where they can spend time with friends and family away from the bustle of city life. It could also provide some valuable rental income. They undoubtedly took on a huge challenge, which was way beyond their skill set or experience, but their good nature and eagerness to learn have afforded them this stylish, modern living space.

LESSONS LEARNT

The boat had neither a mooring nor the necessary licences. These two young brothers, who not only lacked any experience of boats but also fundamental DIY skills, had set themselves a formidable task, but they were not discouraged. Their plan was to work on the boat in the boatyard and to learn as they went along, while looking for a suitable mooring and gaining the necessary boating qualifications and licences.

AIRSTREAM

"We are in love with beauty and a slave to beauty. Honouring the past and defining a new future... the vehicle mirrored that principle. We work to redefine ours and our children's future but look to the wisdom of the past in order to do that."
MARK AND CHARLOTTE

FINDING THAT FIRST STEP ONTO THE PROPERTY LADDER HAS NEVER BEEN EASY. OVER RECENT YEARS THIS HAS BECOME A HERCULEAN TASK FOR MANY YOUNG PEOPLE AND IT WAS NO DIFFERENT FOR MARK AND CHARLOTTE. TOGETHER WITH THEIR YOUNG DAUGHTER, THEY WERE LIVING IN RENTED ACCOMMODATION AND THEIR LEASE WAS COMING TO AN END.

"WE WERE REALLY FED UP WITH THE RENTALS MARKET, BUT IT'S ALSO TRUE TO SAY THAT WE WANTED TO DO SOMETHING A BIT BOLD. RENTING FELT SO MEDIOCRE AND NOT OUR LIFE; WE WANTED TO BE CLOSER TO NATURE AND CONNECTED TO THE LAND. THIS WAS A PROJECT WE COULD PUT OUR CREATIVE ENERGY INTO AND WOULD PROPEL US INTO THE LIFESTYLE WE WANTED."

THE CREATORS
Mark and Charlotte Mabon live in rural Somerset and are both caterers and food educators, working to create healthy and invigorating food which is as fresh, natural, restorative and tasty as possible. They believe that delicious and nutritionally rich food can be available for you, no matter what intolerance or health issue you might have.

THE INSPIRATION
Mark and Charlotte were pondering how to create a more permanent family home with limited means but big principles and a wish for a better life when Charlotte had a dream about a shiny silver Airstream caravan. "In our darkest hour and not knowing what to do we looked at the book *My Cool Caravan* and I dreamt about it." They were so excited by the idea that they started researching it straightaway on the internet and found one for sale on an online auction. A few hours later they set off to a neighbouring county to view it.

Unfortunately, the Airstream wasn't quite right for them, but they got talking to the owner and he had another one for sale that ticked all their boxes. This beast, a 1954 Airstream "Sovereign of the Road", had seen better days and it was a long way from being roadworthy, but the idea of making a home out of it had taken root, and it felt like they were embarking on a real adventure.

THE WORK

The well-worn and battered old Airstream needed some serious work before they could even move it. It had been damaged in an accident and the front quarter section was missing; a new axle was required, together with new brakes and a new tow-hitch; and the chassis needed repairing, too. The man who sold it to them offered his knowledge and experience, and Mark assisted with the work. In addition, they needed professional help to carry out the skilled jobs. Mark describes himself as the lackey, happy to run around and help, source parts and materials, and learn from watching the skilled tradesmen do their jobs.

He took on the challenge of repairing the bodywork himself with help from the seller, who also let Mark carry out this fundamental work in his barn. Repairing the bodywork meant using some identically shaped pieces as templates and cutting the new pieces out of sheet aluminium, learning how to master a rivet gun, and riveting them all into place.

When the structural repairs were complete, they installed a new plywood floor and towed the Airstream back to Somerset. Far from being a terrifying experience, Mark describes that first journey as "amazingly good fun – it was totally empty, so light, and it was a beautiful crystal-clear day. Everyone on the motorway turned their heads."

The walls were the next item on Mark's list to receive his attention. The interior aluminium skin that was riveted to the exterior was removed and the old insulation in between the two layers was taken out. Mark re-insulated it with a more modern aluminium-coated bubble wrap material: an ex-NASA product that is lightweight, has good thermal properties and, importantly, doesn't absorb water, so any water ingress wouldn't be retained by the material.

All this took three weeks of full-on, full days' work. Meanwhile, Mark and Charlotte started thinking about the structure and style of the interior. Mark had conflicted feelings. "It was thrilling and exciting to start visualising how the layout might be. There was quite a lot of sitting around, eating lunch in the caravan, imagining the space and being productive, but working on your own like that you lose a lot of motivation and you really have to push yourself."

THE INTERIOR

The layout of the internal space gradually began to take shape in Mark and Charlotte's minds. Their next step was to bring in their guitar-maker friend, Nathan, to help with the carpentry. They had decided to re-use and re-purpose as much previously used material as possible. And instead of installing new built-in specific pieces, they wanted to buy older ones and customise them to sit well within the idiosyncratic curves of the Airstream.

They looked at online auction sites and made regular trips to their local reclamation yard to source the pieces they needed. They soon accumulated a collection of old items of furniture: a haberdashery unit, fruit and vegetable wooden crates, doors, a bureau, a wood-burning stove, some old glazed tiles... Although they had a layout in mind, they weren't slaves to it and the actual design was refined to work around the pieces they found. They used to stand in the space to get a sense of what would work and what wouldn't.

The exterior look of the Airstream was clearly already spoken for in the inherent glamour of the shiny aluminium, riveted panels and curved, industrial, aerodynamic lines. But inside, the couple wanted to impose their own personal style. Through their readings, the wild goose became a talisman for the project, guiding their way and their spirit and carrying them through the project. They batted backwards and forwards between them possible designs for a wild goose stained-glass window to replace the one missing in the front section bedroom area. Five minutes away, they found a local stained-glass artist to create this for them. Apart from the technical skills that she brought to the

project, she also helped them decide on the gentle colour palette for the piece.

While Mark was working full-time on the Airstream, Charlotte took over the parenting duties and simultaneously began to acquire textiles and vintage fabrics to use inside the caravan. She set up a sewing workroom at home, so she could work on the project while their daughter was having her afternoon naps. Some 1970s navy-blue floral print needle-cord was re-invented and became a small kitchen cupboard curtain hung from a simple net curtain wire. Some vintage grain sacks were made up into simple roll-up blinds for all the windows. Gearing up towards the end of the build, Charlotte began to hand-mix paint colours to use on the interior and exterior of the re-purposed furniture.

THE KITCHEN

It was an absolute pleasure for Mark and Charlotte to work within the restrictions of space and budget. It can be very satisfying when a situation forces you into discovering creative solutions that exceed your requirements and expectations. For instance, they needed some small shelves in the kitchen area for storing dry goods. The walls of the Airstream are not strictly

TEXTILES
Charlotte specially designed a block print pattern for the natural linen to be used as a door curtain for the bedroom.

THE FRIDGE
Amazingly, Mark and Charlotte managed to create their own fridge in a vintage suitcase. The case is lined with vintage wallpaper while an inner aluminium container acts as the actual food box, with a small heat exchanger and fan fitted at the back to cool everything.

vertical and curve gently inwards towards the roof, so a regular narrow shelf screwed into the wall wouldn't work. Instead, they took some spare aluminium from the bodywork repair and formed this into a narrow trough with a lip on the front edge. They made some bits of old leather into small straps to support the shelf at each end and riveted them to the walls. Visually, they loved the mix of aluminium and leather, and let the environment and the materials guide the process and their decisions.

Nathan, the guitar maker, worked his magic on the kitchen, creating the cupboards from reclaimed wood, with heavy wooden old fruit and vegetable boxes as drawers set on sliders. The materials all came from different sources and Mark and Charlotte didn't want a tatty, mismatched finish, so the surfaces were all stained and waxed to create an aged patina and consistent look across the various woods.

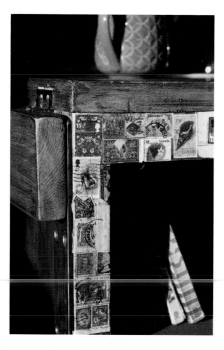

STAMP COLLECTING
Rather than keep their old collection of loose stamps out of sight in a box somewhere they used them as a decorative edging for the shelving unit, each one stuck on with glue and then carefully sealed.

LESSONS LEARNT
They built a shower and a compost toilet even though the plumbing for the shower took Mark an age. He discovered that collecting plumbing parts and fittings of a consistent diameter wasn't easy! They pushed hard to get all the work done in time for the summer. Now he will have the time necessary to prepare the Airstream for the winter, to collect enough wood and to get ready for the cold, wet months ahead.

THE LIVING AREA

They built a curved seating area at the back end of the caravan, with a central-legged table which could be lowered to enable the sofa to become a large additional bed space. Mark and Charlotte made the backrest and large linen padded seat cushions that form the U-shaped unit. Some old Peruvian textiles were divided into two and made into long bolster cushions for added comfort. Charlotte had collected some old leather school satchels and small canvas utility-style bags, and these were fixed along the wooden edge of the seating unit to store small items.

Mark had collected old maps of the area where they live – things of beauty, with their cream-coloured fibrous parchment background, old typeface and elegant fine black lines demarcating the ancient field patterns. He used these as his own highly individual interpretation of wallpaper, trimming them to size and sticking them up with wallpaper paste. It's very engaging to look at exactly where you are on a map, and to imagine how the landscape might have looked and how life must have been many years ago.

The plywood floor was covered in cork tiles with a patchwork of rugs laid on top. An old bureau has been re-used as a working desk, its back legs removed so it can fit snugly over the wheel arches. Its exterior was painted a chalky, matt dove-grey and the interior a rich magenta/fuchsia, both of which were hand-colour-mixed by Charlotte.

Water is supplied from a tank which is replenished by a hosepipe lead once every week or so, and heated by a gas-powered caravan water heater concealed in the box area underneath the sofa. The space is heated by a vintage pale blue highly decorative wood-burning stove, which sits on a slate hearth, and a mixture of old fire-surround tiles from a local reclamation yard were laid as a backplate.

WHERE THEY ARE NOW

The family has moved into the Airstream that is parked in an old apple orchard at the back of a farm where Mark works. At last they have a real home and it has worked out perfectly.

He admits that after the major push on the build he did feel a bit low. He missed the energy and challenge of creating his own home. He feels that "You have got to be ready to lose your life to it in the process." But in the way that many of us feel after a huge project has been completed, he'd now like to do it all again! Undoubtedly, this has been a tremendous amount of work for both Mark and Charlotte, but the end result more than justifies all the hard work they put into the build. For them, the fit feels right and they are really enjoying living there. The lifestyle and sense of permanency that they both craved are now happening.

THE INGENIOUS SEAT

Mark loves to sit on a stool at a countertop, and he really wanted to re-create this in the Airstream, despite the limited amount of available floor space. The idea came to him to design a stool that is hinged to the kitchen counter and swings out when in use. Rather than have it in a regular shape, he designed one based on the gently sweeping curve of a wild goose's neck to reinforce the goose talisman associated with the Airstream. The upholstered stool seat folds flat when it's not in use.

GARDEN SPACES

SHORE COTTAGE STUDIO

MOST OF US ARE FAMILIAR WITH THE EMOTIONAL PULL OF OUR FAMILY HOME, ESPECIALLY THE ONE WHERE WE SPENT OUR FORMATIVE YEARS. FOR LAURA, HER FAMILY HOME IS SOMEWHAT EXTRAORDINARY. IT'S SITED ON A SPECTACULAR BEACH IN THE NORTH OF ENGLAND, TUCKED BENEATH A CLIFF AND IN A LANDSCAPE THAT CAN ONLY BE DESCRIBED AS ABSOLUTELY STUNNING. AND, APART FROM A RUN OF VERY STEEP STEPS UP THE CLIFF BEHIND THE HOUSE, IT IS IN ESSENCE CUT OFF BY THE TIDE TWICE A DAY. WHEN THE OPPORTUNITY CAME UP FOR HER TO MOVE BACK THERE WITH HER OWN FAMILY AND BUILD A STUDIO, SHE JUMPED AT IT.

INSPIRATION STRIKES

Laura's mother, Sue, is an artist and when she bought the property over 30 years ago with her late husband, John, it consisted of two run-down ramshackle cottages. Although it was a well-known local landmark, it was effectively a derelict wreck that had stood empty and exposed to the elements for the previous 30 years. It was a mess, with no ceilings, floors or power.

THE CREATORS

Laura Heath's parents had a pioneering attitude: "Home life was a *Swiss Family Robinson* experience – we were always out, playing on the beach, damming streams, and playing frisbee with Dad. I like to think I'm like my dad; he was really encouraging and always told me to go for it." There's lots of creativity in the family; her mother, Sue, is an artist and her husband, Kris, studied for a fine art degree while being a stay-at-home dad. Laura had a very successful career in academic forensic science, but it felt like she rarely saw her children, and during her third pregnancy she took steps to make some changes.

The family moved in and started the extensive renovation work, camping in the house while rebuilding it around them. Many years later, when Laura, Kris and their two children (with a third on the way) were packing up to leave Shore Cottage for the drive home, Laura told her mother that she didn't want to go. Sue said, "Well, why don't you just live here? It would be lovely." The seed was planted and a little while later Laura was offered a severance package from her employer and the move back home had begun.

THE IDEA FOR THE STUDIO

Sue is a talented textile designer, and working when she had the house to herself wasn't a problem, but with the whole family and grandchildren living there as well she couldn't leave her work stuff lying around. Hence the idea for a separate purpose-built studio was born. Laura and Kris decided to build a working studio for themselves and as a venue for running short art courses. The new space would not only have to work for them as individuals but also for groups who came to develop their artistic skills and learn new ones. The courses would cover creative laser cutting, design stitch, photography and fused glass – a pooling of all of this talented family's wide-ranging skills and crafts.

They identified a space in the garden that could accommodate it, right next to the house. They wisely contacted the planning

department; it became clear that they would require the services of a planning consultant who would be able to help deal with the coastal environmental agency and all other third-party groups concerned with the indigenous wildlife in the area. The planners advised that a bespoke studio would be looked upon more favourably than an off-the-shelf product.

DESIGNING THE STUDIO

It is often hard, even for experienced builders, to grasp fully the relationship between the realities of a space and the measurements on a sketch. The beach became the family's life-size sketchpad and at low tide they drew the plan into the sand and factored their working areas into the space. As Laura says, "It was important that the area flowed and we would all have our own separate working spaces... we ended up with three sinks!"

They started the process, rather like a work of art, by collating

CREATIVE DISPLAYS

Long picture shelves line one wall with a mixture of framed artwork and pieces mounted on driftwood or branches. Even the ceiling is used for utility and display. Ceiling-mounted electrical sockets enable equipment like microwave kilns, sewing machines and laptops to be plugged in without dangerous trailing wires. The display wires suspend beautiful shaped and textured branches, which are used to display small objects or works in progress.

their ideas for shapes and materials in a sketchbook. From looking at other artists' spaces, home offices and garden rooms, it became clear that an off-the-shelf building wasn't going to meet their needs – which coincided with the planners' advice. Instead, they showed their sketchbook to an architect, Mike Jolley, who took on board all their influences, which included Derek Jarman's famous garden at Dungeness, Scandinavian log buildings, and a coastal/maritime theme.

With form following function, they considered the building as a place to work, thinking about how they would use and move through the space. The site itself naturally suggested an L-shaped building. And by drawing the suggested plan out in the sand, they could sit "in" the building in garden chairs, imagining how the space might work, and reconfigure it accordingly. They were careful to account for the true internal measurements of the building being smaller than the external measurements on the plan due to the thickly insulated material required for the walls.

They strove to preserve enough garden space around the studio as well as between it and the house. As they didn't want the studio to overwhelm the space, they decided it was best to site it along the back and side boundaries of the property, leaving a small garden in front. And they needed blank walls within the building to display their artworks – both finished and in progress.

THE BUILD

Based on their specific and detailed brief, Mike worked up a plan that met their needs and took full advantage of this very specific and unique location. The stringent requirements of the planning department meant that the local company hired to fabricate and build the studio had to plan with military precision. The studio was manufactured off-site, delivered and simply slotted together like a big 3D jigsaw on-site. The lorries were precisely loaded so that each piece was unloaded in the correct order for the build.

OYSTERCATCHERS
Laura had an idea to laser-etch a bird design into each piece of the floor. Kris photographed the flocks of oystercatchers that swoop over the estuary and digitally traced their outlines onto the wooden floor tiles. Etching one, two or three floor blocks at a time, Laura could then place them carefully, arranging them in the form of a flock, flying from the entrance door across to the far corner of the studio.

All the wall panels exceeded current insulation requirements in order to maintain a comfortable temperature throughout the year. The floor and ceiling are made from the same panels, and the building stands on Jackpad foundations, constructed out of recycled plastic and steel, thereby avoiding the need for concrete. As well as being better for the environment, this was a practical consideration as it would not have been possible to get a ready-mix concrete lorry down onto the beach, and the only other solution would have been to mix it on-site.

Given the location and the access restrictions dictated by the location and the tide, the planning requirements also deemed that the construction should cause only minimal disruption to the local wildlife and therefore all the deliveries had to be made in a single day. Consequently, they needed a co-ordinated crew including tractors, trailers, telehandlers and associated drivers, to manage the access at low tide across the sandy beach to the site.

At the end of Day Two of the build, the walls and windows were up. After ten days, electricity and water were in place. The large double-glazed windows were custom-made in non-standard sizes to garner the incredible light and the ever-changing scene right in front of them. The studio has a panoramic view of the estuary, which the family wanted to maximise.

ARTISTIC FLAIR

The family's artistic work, whether in laser cutting, textiles or photography, takes its cue from the landscape and features natural materials and textures. It follows that they sought to make every part of the build inspirational, hence having standard fixtures and fittings didn't set their hearts alight. It was important for them that every surface had its own personal artistic touch. Thus the floor needed to be beautiful but also to improve with gradual wear and tear from ground-in beach sand. They settled on reclaimed parquet from a couple of different sources to achieve varying textures and tones throughout rather than a uniform look. Layered on this was a site-specific style of installation. Instead of the parquet being laid in a traditional herringbone, they opted for a gentle wave pattern to echo the mudflats of the estuary at low tide.

The G Plan studio furniture was sourced from local charity shops and their artworks are displayed behind the glass doors of the sleek, mid-century-style units.

Several of the contributors to *Amazing Spaces* appreciate William Morris's adage: "Do not have anything in your home that you do not know to be useful or believe to be beautiful," and with three generations of artists under one roof there are very few things they can't find beauty in!

INNOVATION AND PATRIMONY

As Laura sums it up, "This means everything to us. We could teach anywhere, of course, but working here is outstanding and inspirational. Having the studio allows us to be part of the view and the environment and it has helped us realise [the cottage's] potential. After Dad died, Mum stayed on, but it was getting to the point where she was considering selling up and moving… it would have broken my heart to sell the house. Dad always said that the house should pay for itself, and I think it's starting to now."

LESSONS LEARNT

As this was a completely new, empty space, it was effectively a blank canvas, and Laura and Kris felt strongly that it should be imbued with some history so as not to lack identity or character. They found this could be achieved through sentimental touches and clever up-cycling. "We would have up-cycled even if we had had £1 million to spend on the build. We saved some old school lab benches from a skip years ago and used them in our last house. They're now workbenches in the studio, and we've moved with them three times. Up-cycling just gives the place more personal connection, more heart and soul." Laura's dad's old trunk from when he went away to boarding school is now mounted on castors and makes a fine coffee table, with storage for promotional material for the studio. The teak offcuts from the sink splashbacks have been fixed together and her father's handwriting etched into the surface. It says: "It's your time now, so enjoy it" – poignant words written to Laura when she left for university but equally applicable to anyone visiting the studio for a creative break.

THE WARREN

THE WARREN IS AN UNDERGROUND CHILDREN'S PLAY SPACE IN TAMSIN AND OLI WORTHERSPOON'S BACK GARDEN. THIS AMBITIOUS PROJECT CONSISTS OF A MAGICAL DEN INSIDE A LARGE HOLE, WHICH IS COVERED AND SURROUNDED ON THREE SIDES BY THE EXCAVATED SOIL. THE SOIL HAS BEEN ATTRACTIVELY TURFED SO THEIR KIDS CAN RUN AND RIDE THEIR BIKES OVER THE ROOF OF THE DEN. THE FRONT IS FACED WITH CEDAR SHINGLES, WHICH WEATHER TO A SILVERY GREY, SEAMLESSLY BLENDING INTO THE GARDEN LANDSCAPE.

INSPIRATION AND DESIGN

This project was based on Tolkien's hobbit idyll; Oli and Tamsin both loved the idea of getting together as a family with friends and having a Shire-style party. They wanted to combine a rural, elemental feel with something magical for the children. The Warren would not only be aesthetically pleasing but also other-worldly, sparking their sense of adventure.

When they were planning the style of the build, they purposely didn't refer to *The Hobbit* and *The Lord of the Rings* movies. Sometimes referencing something closely can restrict your thinking rather than liberate it. They wanted to free their minds for something infinitely more creative, but they looked on Pinterest for ideas on how the children could use the space, and the design followed on naturally from this research.

The various aspects of the technical design and its implementation were checked out on YouTube. In addition, Oli sought professional expertise from his father and friends and pooled knowledge and advice wherever it could be gathered. Although this was an unusual project – in reality a mini-build – it had ambition and an enduring appeal that seemed to strike a chord with strangers. The genuine enthusiasm that Oli and Tamsin exuded was met with passion and a keenness to help.

STARTING THE BUILD

The starting block and inspiration for this amazing space was Oli's grandfather, who, many years previously, in a mildly eccentric style, had created a subterranean greenhouse! He had dug a big hole in the garden and put a greenhouse in it. This family's creative roots run deep.

Starting with a rough sketch on a scrap of paper, Oli took a photo of the end of the garden on his tablet. With this image as a base, he started drawing over the top of it, using the Procreate app. He was so enthused that he immediately emailed his sketch to the local planning department and received a fairly encouraging response. Delighted, he developed the drawings in readiness to start work.

THE CREATORS

Like many young parents, Tamsin and Oli wanted to create a happy, safe and relatively free home environment for their six-year-old son and three-year-old daughter. They both trained as art teachers, and after finishing college Oli took a job as a community artist. Part of Oli's brief is to create unique play areas for schools – individual and site-specific little spaces and playground dens – and he liked them so much that he decided to build one in his back garden for his own children. He likes to work in a structured, scheduled way to channel his talents in a purposeful direction and is self-effacing about his combined artistic and practical skills: "Anyone who is artistic is hands-on." He is naturally organised and efficient – qualities that Tamsin appreciates: "I enjoy making things pretty; the fairytale's in my head but things don't happen. Oli makes things happen."

THE STRUCTURAL WORK

Inevitably, shifting large amounts of earth is hard and an onerous task, and not something for the faint-hearted. Oli's father helped him with the heavy and dirty work, and the two of them started work on their mission: to dig a large hole in the back garden.

All the earth from digging the footings and the well to accommodate the pump and sump were piled up to one side to be used later for banking. To take the hard graft out of the digging, they hired a Micro Digger but, as it was too large to manoeuvre through the narrow passageway to the back garden, they had to take it through the house, dirt and all!

The weather was not kind to them and the digging took two days. Watching the rain pour down and the back garden turn into a sea of mud, Oli started to question his judgement. The hole kept filling up with water, so he dashed out and bought an electric pump and, while the rain held off, dug a 66cm (26in)

WILLOW ARCH

Around the entrance path Oli planted an arch of living willow, which, although it started as almost bare branches, is now totally green. He loves creating things like this that fire his children's imagination and teach them about how things grow and change.

PUMPS

Excess water pumped from the sump in the Warren is directed to the other end of the garden. Instead of leaving this area as a wet, soggy mess, Oli linked it to an old wooden whisky barrel, also fitted with a pump, so the kids could play in the water.

circle 1.2m (4ft) deep for the sump. He lined it with an old plastic barrel and lowered the pump into the hole. The pump kicks in automatically when the water reaches a specific level and pumps it out at the other end of the garden.

Oli didn't want the den to be just like a shed – he wanted something far more exciting – but cheerfully admits that he was learning as he went along. The stud walls, made of tanalised outdoor timber, were screwed together carefully. Oli erred on the side of caution due to the amount and weight of the earth going on top and put in a lot of joists, just to be on the safe side. The basic structure was made of timber, wrapped in several layers of Visqueen plastic sheeting before digging down another metre. The timber joists were treated and clad, along with the concrete floor, in untreated OSB board, as in a shed. An access tunnel was installed, together with a skylight to let in some light. Initially, he thought he would need four tonnes of earth to create the illusion that the den is underground, but actually there isn't that much weight on top.

A TEAM EFFORT

A lot of the materials used were found, donated or acquired very cheaply. Oli and Tamsin like to talk to and engage people in their project: to garner knowledge, opinion and advice, to find solutions and ideas as to how to make it work. For instance, they found the ideal piece of piping for the play/escape fun tunnel just outside the workshop, but the big drainpipe for the main tunnel came from a builder's yard. Oli got talking to a man whose yard is near his own, and he liked the project so much that he donated an 2.5m (8ft) piece of heavily constructed pipe – the perfect size and strength – for free. Oli slid it through the mound and wall. Inside there's a lid and a little door – a secret escape that is hidden, and not visible from inside the den. The porthole at the exterior end of the tunnel, where it opens out into the garden on

GEORGE'S OWN BUILD IDEAS AND TIPS

• "Lay a concrete base over the stone base." George advised using two tonnes of hardcore on the mud. The stones can only be bought loose, so bag it up into small bags to carry it round to the back of the house.

• "Use a wheelbarrow to bring 1.5 cubic metres of concrete through the kitchen." It had to be mixed at the front of the house.

• "Create a schedule for the work, especially if you're naturally disorganised." George has to be on schedule for his day job so this has been drilled into him.

• "It's good to have timescales for delivering materials." Otherwise, things can easily slip and it becomes problematic.

• Oli made the stud walling in his workshop, then screwed it onto the base and put this on top of the stone. George advised him to pour the concrete directly over that.

top of the Warren, was bought from an online auction site. Oli wanted a feature aluminium porthole and got his wish; this one came off a ship.

The couple appreciate working with good materials, especially wood, and they tapped into the knowledge and experience of skilled local craftspeople. A local tree surgeon who had taught Oli how to use a chainsaw provided the elm for the door. He had a great understanding of the materials of his trade and was happy to get involved. He proved to be integral to the project, offering advice on the design of the Warren as well as good sources for the best wood to use for each application.

The window and door frame were key to the design, and Oli asked a craftsman who makes timber portholes out of hardwood to produce a much larger version; these became the characterful and beautifully made circular entrance door and window frames in oak.

There isn't a lot of true exterior space with this project, but for around the door at the front of the Warren cedar shingle tiles were slowly and painstakingly cut by hand and provide the finishing touch to the outside. They look deceptively simple but there's an art to doing this. Tamsin found a local man who knew about using shingles and he taught them how to lay them in a distinctive wavy design. As time goes by, they weather to a natural silvery tone.

THE FINISH

Oli had a clear view of how the Warren should sit within the landscape, not wanting it to look too manicured or ornamental. His preference was to create a more natural setting. "I didn't want it packed it out with plants, but wanted it to grow and settle in over time."

Tamsin had a vision in her mind about how she wanted the interior to look and researched this on Pinterest, typing in generic terms, such as "wooden houses." Her plan was to create the atmosphere of a cabin, "One that if you stuck your head outside you might see a unicorn go by…"

She pictured the interior surfaces highly textured to give the walls a rich, warm, woodland feel. Originally, she planned to use shingles on the interior walls as well as the outside, but this proved to be too expensive and time-consuming. However, she still loved the idea of using natural wood for the interior and got thinking about different treatments and applications. She had a Gustav Klimt-inspired plan for the ceiling and adorned it with slivers of tree trunks from Jack the tree surgeon, who had given them so much help and advice.

STAINED-GLASS WINDOW
Set into the front wall is a circular stained-glass window, a piece carefully removed from the porch of their house before it was renovated. Oli had an affection for it from his childhood and got it restored, made the glass secure and fitted it into the shingle wall. Either inside or outside the Warren, the warm light glows through this – it's a timeless, genuine and homely touch.

THE CEILING
Jack the tree surgeon had a supply of interesting woods, including elm, lacewood, cat's paw oak and yew, in different tones, grains and sizes. Over 200 of these were sliced and sanded, the ceiling was painted gold, and the equal-depth circular slices of wood were glued and nailed into place on it, allowing tantalising glimpses of gold to glisten out from between the rounded edges. It's a magical effect.

The films of Tim Burton were another influence on the styling of the interior. Tamsin wanted to emulate his beautiful sense of magic, of unreal things being real, and of proportion being shifted. To this end, Jack came up with a tall tree branch that completely fills a corner opposite the wood-burning stove and appears actually to grow out of the structure of the wall itself, as if nature had found a way of breaking through and inhabiting the interior, too. Tamsin decorated this with fairy lights, tiny lampshades and stuffed woodland creatures – fabulous. For the floor surface, a thick layer of simple bark chips was laid down to continue the hyper-naturalistic look and feel.

At the other end of the Warren, beneath the porthole and the hidden escape tunnel, Oli, Tamsin and Richard the carpenter built a day bed, with an additional pull-out bed in a fairy-tale drawer underneath. Functioning as a seating area or single bed, it is layered with blankets, textiles and cushions.

CHILDHOOD MEMORIES, OLD AND NEW

The plan for the Warren was to combine a natural play space in an environmentally friendly way with the garden landscape and architecture, but Oli wanted it to appeal to adults, too. His passion for working outside, building insect hotels and creating things from pallets and recycled materials is infectious and engaging. As a child, he loved being outdoors, playing games, building treehouses or just being in the open and wants to create the same experience for his children.

Oli and Tamsin live in his grandmother's old house, which is full of childhood memories for him. He enjoyed the freedom of playing in the large garden, swinging from a rope hanging from a tree, and now it seemed like the perfect place to create a more innovative and adventurous interpretation of his natural play dens. He wanted his children to have their own happy memories by building somewhere for them to play, along with their friends, whatever the weather.

Tamsin and Oli weren't fazed by the prospect of very muddy children running in and out of the house and a garden that would suffer the side effects of bikes, footballs, muddy boots and squashed flowerbeds. Oli remembers a friend of his father saying, "Let your children grow and then let the garden grow." The words and the sentiment have stayed with him.

ECLECTIC STYLE

Tamsin happily admits to being a bohemian at heart, and she wanted the space to combine her "hippy roots" with a touch of the Balearic islands, and to make something man-made look as natural as possible. To this end, she collected a mixture of interesting textiles and textures in a loose, confident and comfortable mix.

"The whole feeling is that of excitement... it is one of those points in your life that you look back on, and the amount of fun that we, our children and friends have all had is amazing." OLI

STOVE AND HEARTH

Any cabin-style space seems to demand a wood-burning stove, which somehow adds character and provides a focal point as well as warmth. Oli and Tamsin were given a small stove, which was more than ample for the space, and set it facing the room at an angle on a stone hearth with a twin-walled flue to prevent the children from burning themselves.

GEORGE'S
PROJECT

THE VERANDA

Rather than have the studio end abruptly, we continued the bench seating so that it appears to run through the Perspex door and onto the veranda. There is a continuity of line. The lid of the outside bench lifts up and can be used for storing boots and gardening equipment. But we didn't stop there and we repeated the box shape with the box hedging in the garden.

I BET MOST PEOPLE HAVE LOOKED AT THEIR GARDEN AND THOUGHT ABOUT GETTING A SHED. USUALLY THIS IS A PLACE TO DUMP ALL THOSE SAD REMINDERS OF THE SUMMER: A PADDLING POOL, A MOWER, AN ASSORTMENT OF GARDEN TOOLS AND A BIKE THAT'S NOT USED ENOUGH. OUR GARDENS ARE A HUGE RESOURCE, YET MOST OF THEM ARE SERIOUSLY NEGLECTED. LOOKING AT MY OWN GARDEN, I HAD EXACTLY THE SAME THOUGHTS, PARTICULARLY ABOUT THE OLD SINGLE GARAGE THAT WAS WELL PAST ITS BEST. IT WAS AT THE END OF A NARROW STRIP OF GARDEN AND THE WHOLE SPACE WAS CRYING OUT TO BE BETTER USED. I COULD DO WITH MORE WORK SPACE, THE KIDS NEEDED SOMEWHERE TO DO THEIR HOMEWORK AND HANG OUT WITH THEIR FRIENDS, AND I WANTED A PLACE WHERE WE COULD ALL DO THAT TOGETHER.

THERE HAD TO BE A SOLUTION THAT FELL WITHIN THE PERMITTED DEVELOPMENT RESTRICTIONS, WAS ATTRACTIVE AND WORKED AS A FUN, USABLE SPACE.

THE BRIEF

My own garden isn't huge – it's a typical inner city garden, with houses, other gardens and a mishmash of other sheds and buildings all around. It seemed as though all my neighbours were trying to find a shed-like solution. The garden's an awkward shape, too, with a long tapering section at the back leading to an extremely run-down, tiny, sloping-roofed and falling-to-bits garage stuffed to the gills with the usual domestic paraphernalia.

I have three young children who need space to play, explore, mess about with their friends, and chill out, and even though I'm a great believer in letting children have a sense of freedom, they still need a responsible adult to keep half a watchful eye on them.

THE DESIGN

Talking to my design collaborator and master craftsman, William Hardie, it soon became clear that the starting points would be the narrow and slightly awkward section of the garden and the garage at the end. In order to stay within the permitted development regulations, we couldn't build upwards or outwards, so that little plot of land had to come up with all the answers.

By carrying out a site survey, we had an accurate plan to work from. Like most city gardens, mine couldn't be considered in isolation and I needed to take my neighbours into account. Our solution to the complex requirements of the finished space and existing garage was to create three separate structures, all relating to each other, with multi-functional but specified uses.

The old garage would become a "snug" combining a chill-out space, TV/cinema room, play space and planetarium. It's an odd, almost sculptural shape – angular with a sloping roof and narrowing walls – so it needed a truly individual design solution.

The middle section would be a beautiful Perspex butterfly tunnel. I'm obsessed with butterflies and I've passed this obsession on to my children! The tunnel would add an airy, magical feel while offering a chance to be up close with nature.

Lastly, we wanted a large studio which could open to the sky and feel bright. The aim was to pack in all the multi-functional elements yet for us to be able to move around freely, and then to fold and close everything away neatly when not in use.

Will and I began by making some rough sketches, which, along with the site survey, became the seedbed for our ideas. Will's team developed them further, creating proper drawings for the studio building with CAD (computer-aided design) software. This was the starting point for the really precise and tough work, which was refined repeatedly until we got it right. A plan emerged for my kids and me to have our own fold-down desk and storage area – like a 3D pinboard. Even the fixed sofa seating was put to use. Within this, I wanted a secret snacks and drinks cupboard, but in Will's way of pushing things to the limit, he suggested we use a tiny bit of the space for a pull-out table tennis table!

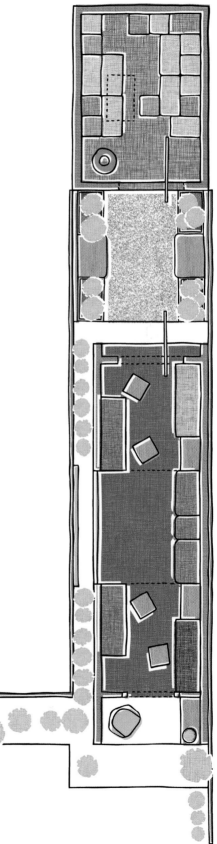

KEEPING THE STRUCTURE SIMPLE

Will's plan was to build the 2.5m (8ft) long studio as a pre-fabricated set of "cassettes" in his workshop, which could then be transported to the site and erected very quickly – in only one-and-a-half hours. These structurally sound and ready-insulated pieces would form the floor, walls and ceiling. Inside each cassette would fit another set of pre-fabricated material, an inner skin containing all the storage, desks, chairs, lighting, a comfortable sofa and some fun elements, too – all hidden within a 110mm (4⅜in) deep cavity in the walls.

The hand-dug foundations would be kept simple: eight concrete pads to support the floor and the weight of the building. The garage would be repaired and refurbished on-site, while the butterfly tunnel was built in the studio from Perspex ready to be installed on-site.

The challenge was to pack all this in, in an aesthetically pleasing way, and to keep it all strictly within the permitted development rules and guidelines. This required a huge amount of effort due to the narrowness of the space. And the specifications of all the materials had to be so hard-working as to remain structurally sound but not eat up too much of that valuable wall space we needed for storage. Even the roof had to have a five-degree pitch for water drain-off, provide enough internal headroom and not exceed the overall permitted height.

STORAGE IN THE STUDIO

Most of the storage in the main studio was hidden within that crucial 110mm (4⅜in) wall cavity. Obviously, that's fine for small items, but large pieces, such as the light box I use for my work, and the rolls of paper I draw on, presented us with a problem, so we addressed each item individually, thinking out a storage method that would work in each instance.

Sometimes this meant storing the items in the vertical on a hinged base that would open to the horizontal. We wanted to use commercially available hardware throughout wherever possible: push catches, hinges, magnets, offset hinges and hooks. However, there was one situation for which we couldn't readily buy the hardware and which needed a bespoke solution, so Will designed and commissioned our own special pivot hinges to support substantial weights. In the main, we strove to source readily available items but to be inventive about their usage.

THE STUDIO ROOF

An electronic movable system was considered for the retractable roof, but a simpler low-tech system was better suited to the purpose: a galvanised "uni-strut" steel hanging system (used for hanging shop lights) was turned upside-down to create a translucent roof that slides open in one direction with a light touch from the inside of the studio.

PLAYING WITH STORAGE

The seating cubes slot back to become part of the linear run of seating along the right-hand side of the studio. When the movable cube seats are in use, the negative space created by them becomes the foot well for the drop-down desks. Next comes a touch of inspired genius using colour and geometry. By designing a 3D impression in a linear shape, the team created a *trompe l'œil* effect: coloured cubes painted on the walls are actually individually shaped cupboard doors for the storage recesses.

THE LARGE WALL IMAGE

We thought long and hard about how to create a sense of space, perspective and a touch of fun in the studio. If you were sitting on the sofa, the view of the inside wall of the studio and through the sliding side door straight onto the garden fence would be dull. The gap between the studio and the fence was only 60cm (23½in), hardly enough to create perspective, but we wanted to give it a go.

I thought of using an image to suggest a notion of perspective – something that would take your eye to the horizon. The ceiling of the studio is Perspex, and, like a light box, it could be gently backlit. In particular, I was keen that whatever image we used would bleed into the ceiling with the same tone and lightness, so there wasn't a massive visual leap between the two.

We decided to shoot the image ourselves to ensure that the composition worked for the space. This was vital as its centre would be on the fence, and it would only be visible in full when the sliding door was open. Brighton seafront seemed perfect – the Palace Pier is the main structure and its strong architectural interest runs from the right into the middle of the image, with a strong perspective as it extends into the sea. You don't feel that you're only a few centimetres away from your neighbour's fence.

ADDING LIGHT AND PERSPECTIVE
By having the end walls of the studio clear
and made of Perspex, it was possible not only
to get an incredible amount of light into each
structure but it also made the aspect line up,
so from the French doors at the back of the
house you could see the entire length of all
three buildings. The circular doors between the
rooms were another welcome eureka moment.
They have an element of magic, an excitement
and a subtle message that you are entering a
fantastical place; whether it's a sci-fi spaceship
or sculptural felt-lined snug, there's no doubt
that this goes beyond the ordinary.

*"It's not until you set
yourself a challenge that
you find you can surprise
yourself. This is a simple
garden space and I have
found it an inspiration."*

THE SNUG

The style of the snug was informed by the shape and qualities of
the garage in which it was created; the space naturally suggested
a warm and cosy ambience. From a practical point of view, the
snug needed to work as a daytime play space yet become totally
blacked out when it was functioning in cinema and planetarium
mode. The room is a peculiar shape and the idea was to cover
it entirely in fabric to make it really soft and cosy, and to work
within a contained colour palette so the space is seen as a whole.
When the building had been made dry, the walls and ceiling were
lined in felt-covered plywood panels and the floor was carpeted.

Inspired by children's building blocks, we developed a plan
to create a multi-functional playful space, utilising felt-covered
large blocks in varying sizes, which all relate to each other. These
could be used variably as staged seating in cinema mode, in the
creative play zone as building blocks, and as a massive bed totally
covering the floor when the snug was in planetarium mode.

THE BUTTERFLY TUNNEL

Occasionally, just occasionally, we get the chance to fulfil our
dreams. The tunnel could be perceived as an indulgence but

as my kids and I love butterflies, I talked to some experts and realised I could create my own on a small scale. Set between the studio and the snug, it would create a completely different mood and feel. The snug is cosy, the studio is purposeful and fun, and in contrast, the butterfly tunnel is pure beauty.

Design-wise, it gave us a chance to add a contrast to the shapes of the buildings on either side of it, so I gave Will a challenge: take five days to see what you can think up and make. Inspired by the geodesic domes of Buckminster Fuller, grid-shell structures, traditional boat-building techniques, polytunnels and yurts, Will's ideas morphed via a sketch on an envelope, and with uncharacteristic rashness we just went for it!

Constructed out of oak slats fixed to big oak sills, the structure was clad in Perspex, with an opaque, curved roof section and a fine gauze liner so that the butterflies didn't get too hot. The floor was covered in pea shingle. From a farm shop we bought two metal cattle troughs to accommodate butterfly-friendly plants, and two seats were made to sit on top of each trough.

SPACE TO BREATHE Trying to avoid making the studio seem cramped was a huge technical challenge: shaving millimetres off walls wherever we could yet keeping it structurally sound wasn't easy. However, we succeeded and although it isn't a large area, internally it feels surprisingly spacious.

LESSONS LEARNT

It takes a certain mental discipline to think and rethink; to look at a specific issue and not just accept the first solution as the best one. Also, I've discovered that applying the big thinking to the small details is particularly valid. When they work well collectively, all those seemingly inconsequential details add up to a successful building, and in a small space it's the minutiae that really count. Take, for example, the depth of a seat or a desk flap: the extra millimetre claimed as potential storage space is a minor victory, and in terms of the room's use this can be crucially important. Will and his team's approach was to play, play and play again with ideas to achieve a building that was as lean as possible, materially and design-wise.

INSTALLATION

A major issue for us with this project was that there was little space around the studio and butterfly tunnel. The back wall of the studio was tight up against the garden fences and neighbours' boundaries, so the whole structure had to be installed from the inside rather than from outside. There was no exterior access available for the cassettes to be fitted. We needed to think all that out in the design stages in Will's workshop.

The cassettes were fabricated ahead of time so that all the layers were in place and could be installed in one go: the exterior cladding, waterproofing, structure and insulation.

The roof of Tata steel was a lightweight affordable solution and worked well with the retracting, movable multi-cell polycarbonate roof system with a folded steel frame. With a C-shaped section and wheels, the roof light would be extremely stable and wouldn't lift in the wind.

It seemed sensible to adopt the same system and materials for the sliding side door for the studio, too.

MATERIALS

Using everyday materials from regular builders' merchants was, in many ways, quite liberating: we avoided spending hours and lots of money sourcing exactly the right product. Instead we set ourselves the challenge of using the commonplace and elevating it. We used two woods: Far Eastern plywood, which is available just about anywhere, treated with dyes and oils to a warm mid-tone. And we also mixed it with elm to make the movable box stools and cupboard doors as well as the big sections around the side and ceiling door openings, and on the places that needed a visible trim, such as around the wine-glass holders and table tennis table legs.

THE GARDEN

To make the narrow gap between the studio and the fence seem bigger and to add a sense of fun and adventure for the kids we decided to cover the whole length of the studio with a mirror. On one of our inspirational journeys for the Treehouse project (p104), we visited the mirror-covered tree house in Sweden. I guess some ideas lurk in the back of your mind, waiting for the right opportunity, and this really did feel like the right approach. I was pleased with how this simple touch transformed that narrowest of spaces.

In this alley we emulated the Brighton beach shingle image by using the same material on the ground, with small areas of planting – a gesture towards the naturalistic look of those tough seaside plants that seem to survive in all weathers. The access to the alley was planted with a small line of bamboo to create a secret walkway, as if this were a hidden space, waiting to be explored.

I wanted the garden to feel modern and architectural, and planned to achieve this by using a limited range of plants, but in large multiples. The kids would still need some lawn, but tall flowing areas of grasses, neat clipped box plants and espaliered trees don't take up much room along the fenced perimeter.

I love this space. It not only makes me smile every day looking at it from my house, but I love its architecture, its colour and light, too. If the kids had their way they would stay out there until midnight. It's not only fun for them but now we all have a place where we can hang out together, play table tennis, do some model making or drawing or simply muck about.

THE DESKS

The kids and I have our own coloured, personalised desk where we can work with and get inspired by items stored in the back. There is additional storage in the cupboards surrounding each desk, and by using clever design and easily available mechanisms there is enough space to store all the items needed, such as paint, paper, stationery, glue, reference notebooks and toys. It's great to open a desk, pull up a stool and have everything to hand.

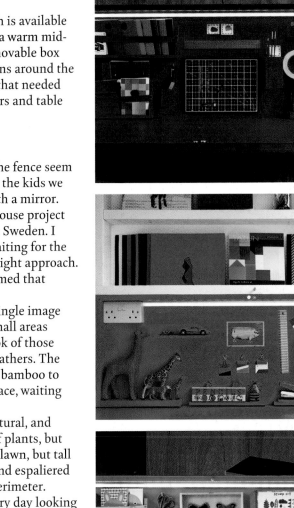

WORK SPACES

THE CREATORS

Simon Bowden works full-time for a local artisan cheese company and dreams about owning his own restaurant one day, or buying a plot of land and retail premises to develop his own deli or food-related business. Before he and his wife, Rachael, can do that, they need to save up some money, and they were inspired by a money-making project they began a couple of years ago – selling ploughman's lunches and artisan cheeses in picnic form at festivals and events.

THE WHOLE CHEESE

FOR SIMON, THE WHOLE CHEESE IS THE FIRST STEP IN ACCOMPLISHING A LONG-HELD AMBITION. BY CREATING AN AFFORDABLE, TRANSPORTABLE AND FLEXIBLE BUSINESS AS A CHEESEMONGER, HE HOPES THAT OVER THE NEXT TWO YEARS HE WILL NOT ONLY BE ABLE TO START SAVING FOR HIS "BIG PROJECT" BUT HE WILL ALSO FULLY RESEARCH THE MARKET, HAVE SOME FUN, AND DEVELOP HIS IDEAS ALONG THE WAY.

THE PROJECT

Without making a huge financial commitment, Simon and his wife, Rachael, had previously gauged the market by trading very simply from a canvas gazebo and some trestle tables. Simon knew that people wanted and expected good food at festivals – and, not surprisingly, they liked it. The time had come to invest modestly in the next stage of the business, and to find a more convenient means of trading, which was quicker to set up on arrival. The horsebox was the ideal means of fulfilling this.

THE HORSEBOX

For those in the know, Rice horseboxes are respected for their classic design and sturdy construction. Simon and Rachael spotted this 1970s one on an online auction site; it fitted their brief and, as Simon says, "It was meant to be – it was literally down the road." He bid on it right up to the deadline against another interested party, but in the final seconds the horsebox was his. It was in its original state, with a tiny jockey seat inside, a hay loft for the horses and low-tech but sturdy and practical fittings. This was a highly functional and uncomplicated vehicle. There were two ramps, one at the back and the other at the side, as well as a small doorway. Simon's plan was to use the rear ramp for access, leave the horsebox features intact, and create a space that could double up as additional storage or an overnight sleeping platform when the horsebox was not in use.

THE BUILD

The horsebox had two big advantages: it was extremely sturdy, as it had been built to carry two horses of an approximate total two-tonne weight: and it was towable behind a suitable vehicle. The chassis was good, and a new plywood floor had been installed. On the downside, there were a few spots of rust, and it suffered from the common problem of ammonia damage from horses' urine in parts of the interior. For these reasons, repairs were carried out, another plywood floor installed, the gaps were repaired and the rust sanded down and treated.

THE SLEEPING AREA
Simon has ingeniously used one of the original ramps of the horsebox to create additional floorspace which can be used as a sleeping area when the horsebox is not in cheese-selling mode, or as additional storage when it is. When the ramp is flat, a simple waterproof covering folds down to create a roof over the area and is secured by a simple bungee cord that fits over the wooden base.

Simon's plan was to keep things relatively simple and retain the original paintwork and overall look. The exterior would be left intact, apart from the serving hatch he had fitted.

Internally, Simon built a storage loft, which was fixed to the ceiling and accessible from both ends, plus two narrow counters that run along each side of the van. Again, he wanted to ensure that the design and materials were in keeping with the horsebox itself: simple finished wood, scaffolding poles and fixings, a stainless-steel, small-bowl sink, and a storage shelf area fashioned from old wooden wine boxes (donated by a friend who works in the wine trade) set on their sides and supported by more scaffold poles. The pub opposite his house was throwing out an old under-counter fridge, so that got recycled and found a new home in the van, too. The new venture was nearly ready to go.

The horsebox is now fully set up to travel and sell cheese, and it's a charming and engaging project. It is delightfully low-tech, and has an engaging pastoral feel that echoes the look of French rural farmers' markets.

THE SERVING HATCH

A hatch for the serving area was cut into a side wall of the vehicle. In his search for a tradesman to create the hatch, Simon looked first at camper-van conversion companies, but "most of them were busy for about a year". Consequently, he researched companies that built and worked on trailers and could create a simple swing-up opening hatch, supported by gas struts and a safety bar.

LESSONS LEARNT

Although he has never done anything like this before, Simon is pleased with the outcome. There are a few modifications that he would make if he were to do it all again, but that's not unusual and I think many of us feel like that at the end of a project; there's always room for improvement.

GLORIA, THE HORSEBOX CLOTHES SHOP

SINCE CHLOE HAD LONG LOVED VINTAGE CLOTHES AND ENJOYED DEALING WITH CUSTOMERS, SHE PLUCKED UP THE COURAGE TO EMBARK ON HER OWN COMMERCIAL ENTERPRISE USING BOTH HER TALENTS AND HER INTERESTS. SHE STARTED A COMPANY CALLED "CRYSTAL VINTAGE", NAMED AFTER HER GLAMOROUS AND INSPIRING GRANNY. "I NEEDED A NEW DIRECTION THAT INCORPORATED MY PASSION AND SKILLS, WAS DO-ABLE AS A SINGLE MUM, AND THAT WOULD INSPIRE MY GIRLS ENOUGH FOR THEM TO COME ALONG FOR THE RIDE. VINTAGE CLOTHES WAS A NATURAL PATH."

THE CREATOR

Chloe LeFay had worked as a dance teacher in Austria and decided to move back to the UK. She was a single mum and had two young daughters. Over the years, she had done a good deal of styling for friends in bands or in the theatre and she had a large collection of vintage clothes herself.

THE MOTIVATION

It occurred to Chloe to buy a vehicle to use principally as a mobile shop for driving around festivals, fairs or even just to see clients. But she could also have a small area sectioned off for the family to use as a camper van.

Driving home one day she spotted an old wooden horsebox sitting in a muddy puddle. It was in a yard next door to where her brother-in-law lives. The owner had planned to restore the 2004

horsebox but it had never happened, and he agreed to sell it to Chloe. Her brother-in-law then offered to carry out the necessary maintenance work to get it roadworthy and successfully through its MOT test.

THE RENOVATION

Besides the area in which the two horses in transit would have been accommodated, there was also a front camper and kitchen section. This was in fairly good condition, just needing general renovation, and the seating and beds would have to be re-upholstered and recovered.

The girls named the 7.5-ton horsebox after the Patti Smith cover "Gloria", and although it had the allure of bygone glamour, it was in truth a muddy, rusty mess. The plan was to restore and convert it using only reclaimed or recycled materials and what already existed inside, and power would be supplied via solar panels.

Access to the shop section of the box is via ramps at the back and sides. The interior is lined in a linear patchwork pattern of scrap-wood strips and vintage drawers and shelving, and the vintage clothes are hung along each side of the van on blacksmith-made iron rails. Vintage mannequins and hat stands sit on shelves on the partition wall between the shop and the front camper-van section.

ON THE ROAD

Now finished, Gloria is a fine-looking beast of a truck: black and stately on the outside and full of vintage treasures on the inside. Chloe is busy taking the truck around vintage events and festivals, and Gloria is loved everywhere she goes. The horsebox has provided Chloe and her girls with a new lifestyle, and experiences that the girls will take with them.

MOBILE CINEMA

THE CREATOR
During his final year of a visual arts degree, Ollie Halls specialised in projection-based installation before an idyllic period of travelling and living on the road in a converted Bedford bus. From Ibiza to Somerset, he worked on cash day-jobs, finally returning to England in 2002 when he began doing contract work at music festivals. It was during this period that he started to produce cinema shows for his co-workers, projecting the image from the back of his Bedford bus *Cinema Paradiso*-style onto the side of a well-positioned white painted truck. A chance conversation one night led to someone suggesting that he buy a custom-made mobile cinema – and that's how he acquired this incredible piece of history.

THE SIGHT OF THIS BUS EVOKES THOUGHTS OF A VERY DIFFERENT TIME: OF POST-WAR AUSTERITY AND THE EXCITEMENT OF FUTURISTIC SPACE-AGE DESIGN. COMMISSIONED BY THE LATE TONY BENN WHEN HE WAS APPOINTED MINISTER OF TECHNOLOGY IN 1966, THIS BUS WAS ONE OF ONLY SEVEN MADE. AS PART OF THE NEW "PRODUCTION ENGINEERING ADVISORY SERVICE", ITS PURPOSE WAS TO TOUR GREAT BRITAIN, VISITING FACTORIES TO SCREEN GOVERNMENT INFORMATION FILMS ABOUT ADVANCES IN INDUSTRIAL TECHNIQUES, MECHANISATION AND AUTOMATION PROCESSES, AND HEALTH AND SAFETY. HOWEVER, IN 1970 WHEN EDWARD HEATH BECAME PRIME MINISTER, THE BUSES WERE NO LONGER DEEMED NECESSARY AND THEY WERE DECOMMISSIONED.

THE BUS, PAST AND PRESENT
In the 30-odd years since its manufacture, the bus has lived through many lives: as a vehicle for promoting the repatriation of *The Flying Scotsman* from its recent spell down under in Australia; as a piece of transport heritage preserved by the national charity Transport Trust; and as a hobby for bus enthusiast Peter Rawley.

Through a circuitous route, another enthusiast, Ollie, purchased the bus, and he was determined to get the old dear not only back into good shape but back to work, too.

THE SEATS
The seats came from an old cinema via a reclaimed materials yard, and these, more than anything else, really set the tone for the interior. All the other fixtures and fittings that were brought in – the lights, doors and furniture – were led by the design of the seats.

"This bus generates a lot of love." OLLIE

A STEP BACK IN TIME
The bus's original projection system was obsolete, so Ollie installed an Epson digital projector and Dolby 7.1 surround-sound system. Mostly, he plays DVDs to his clients, but he has screened a 16mm film in the bus: "It's much more soulful."

THE RESTORATION

Ollie applied to the Film Council for a grant to run a North Devon Movie Bus that would tour the county showing film projects and adding "the cool factor" to local school and community events. It could also generate income by being rented out to private business clients and TV companies. The grant was approved and this spurred him to embark on the restoration.

When he acquired the bus, it was in a sorry state: the engine had seized up, the gearbox had been stolen, the brakes were stuck, and the mechanics were not in good shape. Inside, it was an empty shell, and the original sloping floor – the raked stage of the cinema – had to be reinstated. Ollie found a local tradesman to make one out of aluminium for a reasonable price. The original seating plan had been for 26 people but it felt cramped, so Ollie went for more legroom and fitted 22 instead.

The bodywork, inside and out, was in very good condition: the trim was intact and all the original features remained, so the only work needed was a paint job.

The wiring for the original bus was still intact and functioning, although the original projector electrical wiring had fallen prey to sharp-toothed squirrels. The new special 8.25 x 20 tyres on the bus were ordered and the engine was entirely replaced with one from a Bedford horsebox with only 40,000 miles on the clock.

Next, Ollie had to make the cinema bus functional rather than an interesting museum piece, so he installed a new projection system. Now complete, this unique and atmospheric vehicle has an amazing new lease of life.

THE
OPTICIAN'S
HUT

FOR NATALIE, DEVELOPING THIS UNIQUE STUDIO AND SHOP CONCEPT IN HER OWN NEIGHBOURHOOD IN EAST LONDON WAS A LONG TIME IN THE MAKING. BY MELDING HER KNOWLEDGE OF OPHTHALMOLOGY WITH HER CREATIVE TALENTS AND WEAVING THE TWO TOGETHER, NATALIE CONCEIVED A PLAN OF SETTING UP HER OWN VINTAGE OPTICIAN'S SHOP AND FLEDGLING BUSINESS CONCERNED WITH DESIGNING AND MANUFACTURING VINTAGE-STYLE FRAMES.

THE EPIPHANY

Having made the decision, Natalie started looking for a suitable location for her start-up business. It came as no surprise that the investment needed to set up a conventional town-centre shop can be prohibitively expensive, but her local neighbourhood in Hackney provided a possible solution. It has long been a place of change and regeneration, shaped by many different cultures. Natalie looked around for inspiration for both the style of her business and a suitable location. Her epiphany came when she noticed the local churches: some were grand, cathedral-style buildings while others were more informal, small-scale "tin tabernacles" – charming kit-built churches made of simple corrugated iron. She realised that both types of building served the same purpose and were equally valid, and this was enough to convince her that small, carefully considered and hand-built were the right way to proceed.

A traditional high-street shop wasn't an option but Natalie saw the possibility of creating her own pop up-style permanent shop in one of London's hip inner-city markets which encourage the development of local businesses. For her, this was the creative and fashionable Netil Market in Hackney – a small site squeezed in by an overhead railway line where similar burgeoning businesses, cafés, bike repair shops, bars, jewellers and florists were already up and running. Her initial idea was to base the shop in a vintage caravan and the market's management team loved the idea, but it felt temporary and a permanent building would be more reassuring to customers. Things were starting to take shape.

COLLECTING THE STOCK

Most glasses sold have modern-style frames, but many of the businesses in which Natalie worked had old, retro stock gathering dust in the recesses of their stockrooms. Many owners were keen to move this dead stock and to sell it on to Natalie. The word soon got around to suppliers and optician's shops going out of business that there was someone who wanted to buy their redundant vintage stock. She also started collecting their vintage shop fittings – mannequin heads, ornaments and general display cases – and tested the market by taking a stall at a friend's yard sale. Her goods were so popular that she made more sales and profit than anyone else.

THE SHOP DESIGN

Natalie's initial design was a sketch on a Post-It note – a simple, oblong wooden structure with a glazed, quasi-bell tower. During her student days working in optician's shops, Natalie had observed that customers seemed to value plenty of natural light – hence the bell tower would let in a soft top light from all four sides. The shop would have two windows and a central glazed double door at the front, with a small covered veranda. Natalie knew that all her friends would love to stop by for a chat, so here was a place they could talk and hang out without crowding out the shop! And opening the shop front onto the market scene would encourage potential customers to engage with and enter the space. Eventually the design was worked up properly, but that

BELL TOWER
Not only does the bell tower let in plenty of light, it is also a nod to the makeshift tin chapels found in the neighbourhood.

"People walk in, look up and say that a lot of love went into this building... it makes them smile." NATALIE

early vision had got her a long way and the eventual design didn't change radically.

She started by getting quotes for building the structure from scratch, or buying it ready-made. Neither option was affordable, and although she had absolutely no building experience she persevered, took on the challenge and found a way to make it work. That tiny first sketch was enough to get the ball rolling, and Natalie started telling people about her plan. Being a kindly and creative bunch, they loved this artistic yet practical venture and offers of help started to flow in from friends who had some practical knowledge; a local tree surgeon, for example, kindly donated two tree trunks to support the veranda roof. The plan was to build a safe, core frame structure using new timber while the rest of the cladding materials for the building, including windows and doors, were a motley collection of items found in skips or on donated goods websites.

The actual build took only three weeks to complete and was a collective project with all of Natalie's friends, including Adam, a painter and decorator, and even other people from the market and vague acquaintances contributing to the group effort. Their building skills were rudimentary and any specific skills that were lacking were learnt from YouTube videos – they were all on one huge learning curve.

THE INTERIOR

Natalie had been imagining the interior look of the shop for a long time: it would have a quirky yet welcoming vintage aspect. Many of her collected old optician's shop display items would have a new home, and all the furniture would be vintage.

Her sister designed and printed a special wallpaper, based on hand-drawn scenes of the locality. This space would have character, individuality and charm – as far removed from the homogeneous, clinical-looking chain-store opticians as Natalie could make it.

The vintage frames sit in old display cases or on period-style mannequin heads and a row of 1940s and '50s household mirrors hangs on the wall for customers to use. The light and the space work very effectively: there's room to move around and take in this characterful shop.

LOOKING FORWARD

The business took off immediately, despite the hut being open only three days a week. Natalie utilises Thursdays and Fridays as her design time, drawing up ideas for her own range of vintage-style spectacle frames. The hut is open on those days by appointment and customers enjoy the one-on-one attention they receive. With her skilled, aesthetic eye, Natalie discerns which frame shapes work best for everyone's face shape and personal style. On Saturdays when the market is in full throng, all the shops are open and it's a busy and sociable space, with the deliciously homely veranda always busy. Natalie's plan is to let it change and develop naturally over time, adding items as she finds them and making bespoke pieces when the situation allows.

UP-CYCLING
In keeping with the recycled and secondhand nature of the shop's décor, Natalie's design desk and chair, sited in the good light of the window and welcoming for customers, has been up-cycled and lends yet more character to the space.

SUZANNE AND ANDY ARE PEOPLE OF GREAT CHARACTER WHO HAVE SPENT THEIR ENTIRE CAREERS IN PUBLIC SERVICE, WORKING SHIFTS AND FITTING IN THEIR FAMILY LIFE AROUND THEIR WORK. NOW THEY ARE MAKING PLANS FOR A DIFFERENT KIND OF FUTURE. THIS IS ONE OF THOSE PROJECTS WHERE SEVERAL STRANDS OF INFLUENCE FROM DIFFERENT FAMILY MEMBERS WEAVE TOGETHER TO PRODUCE AN IDEA THAT IS THE PERFECT FIT FOR THE OWNERS. THEY LIVE IN THE WEST OF ENGLAND, FAMED FOR ITS GREEN AND GENTLE COUNTRYSIDE AND DELICIOUS CREAM TEAS. THEY LIKE TO TRAVEL AROUND THE AREA AND HAVE ALWAYS ENJOYED STOPPING OFF FOR SCONES, JAM AND CLOTTED CREAM. AND NOW, THEY HAVE MADE THEIR DREAM COME TRUE BY TURNING THIS INTO A SPECIAL BUSINESS.

THE CREATORS

Suzanne and Andy Ware are now in the latter stages of their careers – Andy as a policeman, Suzanne looking after people with severe learning difficulties. For them, there has never been a better time to look for an alternative working environment. They describe their working and family life up until now as "ships that pass in the night. We have grown to appreciate the more tranquil harmonies of life and really want to spend some quality time working and relaxing together and being more in control of our destiny."

CREAM-TEA CAMPER

BREWING A PLOT

As part of his police work, Andy spent many hours out on patrol in lovely rural locations, noticing what was going on and policing countryside events. It was then that he had the idea for the business, and started to develop a proper business plan.

He and Suzanne talked with their family and friends and, without exception, the feedback from everyone was positive and the idea took root. In the end, it was Andy's dad, Allan, who really channelled his drive and enthusiasm into the project, and they started to look at the logistics of how a business like this might work. "We did our research on the internet, looking at what similar businesses were trading. We scoped all the potential trading environments available and agreed that vintage was the key. We then started looking at vehicle options."

THE VEHICLES

The vehicles they found were advertised on a national auction site and for Andy and Suzanne, shortly followed by Allan, "It was love at first sight." The caravan had been sourced by the previous owners to complement a camper van as a combined unit for a vintage-themed family wedding event.

"Daisy" is a 1987 Volkswagen camper van, and "Lu", the caravan, is a two-berth touring Thomson Mini-Glen, made in the 1960s. Suzanne tells the story: "Andy happened to mention the vehicles in conversation to his dad, and from that point onwards Allan became an integral part of the build. The vehicles were for

HIDDEN TALENTS

The tiered cake stands are a distinctive feature of the teas that the couple serves. In fact, Andy manufactures them himself, a skill he learnt along the way.

sale in Coventry, a four-hour drive away, so they took a trip up there, checked them over, gave them a test drive, reviewed their mechanical history and took a chance with the rest. Two trips to Coventry later, we brought Daisy and Lu home."

PEOPLE SKILLS

Although neither of them had any direct catering experience, Andy and Suzanne weren't deterred. Suzanne had loved baking ever since her childhood years spent with her late grandmother and she can make "a mean sponge". Before joining the police service Andy had pursued a successful management career in retailing. Above all, they are both accustomed to working in the public eye, dealing with people and chatting comfortably with them – an undisputed asset when running a public-facing business. As they say, "We are both very sociable people and have strong spiritual beliefs."

Andy believes that to succeed in business you need a great product, excellent customer-service skills and a unique idea, all of which this enterprising couple has.

BESPOKE AWNING
To provide some shelter for their customers, Suzanne found a company in the United States that was able to make an awning to their specification in colours that worked with the paintwork on the camper and caravan. It's a vintage sun-shade style with a scalloped edge.

LESSONS LEARNT

The renovations were carried out over a six-week period and within their projected budget and contingency spend. Even then they could not hit the road. The vehicles had to be registered with the environmental health authorities and the local council, and were assessed and rated. In addition, as they are providing food products there was a legal requirement for them to undertake food hygiene training; they had to be patient before starting their engines.

THE BUILD

Andy sketched a floor plan for the caravan, researched the fabric and also made a working model for the serving hatch.

Allan had been a builder for the duration of his working life, and his skills were key to making this project happen. They complemented Andy's own expertise and business mind. Meanwhile, Suzanne's flair and eye for the practicalities of service were exacting, and she would not be moved on her decisions about the internal layouts; time proved that she was absolutely correct in her vision.

Electric power was already installed but subsequently upgraded to accommodate all the appliances that would be in use. The gas supply was removed as this was not deemed necessary for the business and had the potential for unseen problems. Both vehicles were stripped bare and the design and build were developed as they went along. However, the basic layout, as originally planned, remained relatively unchanged. Between the two vehicles, there needed to be the facilities to cook, prepare and store food as well as to serve it and seat people comfortably.

INTERIOR DESIGN

In terms of the style, the couple wanted a vintage, retro theme from the outset and they tried to source original materials, such as the kitchen units and wall coverings. However, their selection was dictated by other factors, such as weight ratios, which were a consideration in every aspect of the build.

For the sitting area, they purchased a number of decorative items at the beginning of the project. Since then, charity shops, car-boot sales and local buy-and-sell sites have all turned up an assortment of treasures.

A NICE CUP OF TEA AND A SIT DOWN

Andy and Suzanne have put a great many years into helping others but they are now gearing up to this next adventure when they can enjoy working and spending time together. Thinking about this entire project, it is great to see how this family has really pulled together, helped each other and got involved with making this a success. This camper van and little caravan combo is an absolute delight.

HOLIDAY SPACES

THE BIG GREEN BUS

"The bus is a very peaceful place and it has a great vibe. I think it's because so many people have been on it over the years. People who've fallen in love, argued, slept, cried and laughed on it... some may even have been conceived on it, who knows? It has carried a great many souls." ADAM

THERE AREN'T MANY OF US WHO WOULD EMBARK ON A BIG PROJECT WITHOUT THE ESSENTIALS OF: THE FINANCE TO DO THE JOB; ANY EXPERIENCE; THOROUGH AND DETAILED PLANNING; AND A CLEAR IDEA OF EXACTLY WHAT WE WANTED TO ACHIEVE. BUT, FORTUNATELY, ADAM ISN'T LIKE THE REST OF US. HAVING WANTED HIS OWN HOLIDAY ACCOMMODATION FOR A WHILE, THE SPARK OF AN IDEA CAME IN A FLASH ONE DAY WHEN ADAM WAS ON THE ROAD DRIVING HOME FROM VISITING HIS PARENTS. PASSING A FARM, HE SPOTTED AN OLD CLASSIC ROUTEMASTER BUS IN A FIELD. THE SEED WAS SOWN, AND ON THE SPOT HE DECIDED TO LOOK INTO BUYING ONE AND TURNING IT INTO HOLIDAY ACCOMMODATION FOR HIMSELF AND HIS FAMILY.

AN ADVENTUROUS SPIRIT

Adam's first thought was to buy a run-down property, but even tiny houses without a roof were well out of his price range. When the bus concept occurred to him, he launched right in. Adam's character and practical skills, and the fact that he didn't have to mortgage his house to give this a go, meant there was just a chance that it might work out. By following his instincts and applying good practical knowledge, this step-by-step free-form approach seemed like an adventure that might have spectacular and life-changing results.

Adam knew he wanted to create something really good but,
as he says – and hold on to your hat while you read this – "I was
looking to create something special. I knew that, but I didn't
know how much it would cost. I only knew that I didn't have
enough to finish the project before I started it." Foolhardy or
brave and inspired? Take your pick.

BUYING THE BUS

When it came to sourcing the right bus, Adam had luck on his
side. Secondhand double-decker buses were relatively well priced.
However, he later realised why – they really are quite big, and
parking them isn't easy, so they have only a limited market. He
managed to find a 1982 MCW Metro Bus for £4,500 and took it
for a short test drive around a local industrial estate. Only a week
earlier, it was in service around the streets of Birmingham.

Adam looked at the mileage: 675,000 miles – more than the
distance from the earth to the moon and back. The bus came with
a 12-month MOT test certificate, but Adam still had a lot of work
to do on it as well as needing to find some land where he could
keep the bus.

Having bought the bus, he needed to get it home, so he
arranged to meet the ex-owner at a service station halfway along
the 180-mile route between their different locations. They were
going to take it in turns to drive the bus, so that Adam could

THE BOLD KITCHEN

Adam chose to cover the doors with a vivid green Perspex and add a solid oak worktop. "It was the cheapest kitchen I could get. I like the fact I made something look rich that wasn't. The mix-and-match philosophy worked well, and it's like wearing a pair of designer jeans with a shirt from a supermarket."

THE SHOWERS

Downstairs there is a separate small bathroom/ wet room, while outside is an outdoor shower that works on a timer mechanism, like the ones in gyms and swimming pools. "It's great as it's a larger space, so if you're bigger or taller it works perfectly; the inside shower is a bit tight." The outside shower area is semi-enclosed and has a decking floor.

master the skills under supervision. But things didn't run to plan; the owner had to head back for a meeting, so Adam set off on his own. Thankfully, both he and the bus made it home in one piece.

The next issue to arise, unforeseen thanks to Adam's blind enthusiasm, was where to keep the bus and work on it. To find a quick solution, he turned to social media and Tweeted "Help – I've bought a bus – has anyone got any land?" The local newspaper picked up on the story in their page-three feature, "Weird and Wacky Local Stories" and, lo and behold, an offer came from a local riding school that had space. For a modest rent, Adam could keep the bus there and work on it.

THE CONVERSION

Having confidence, combined with a will not to embarrass yourself, means that you can achieve a great deal, albeit by default. Adam had talked the talk with his friends, telling them that he was going to carry out a high-quality conversion. However, as soon as he started the work he realised that he had set himself high standards and the renovation would have to be as good as he'd told everyone it was going to be. As he says, "I'm a tradesman as well, so I knew how to do everything, and there was no point in asking anyone else to help. Also, it was my project. I couldn't expect others to share my level of enthusiasm."

THE LAYOUT

In design terms, the upper deck was simple. Adam just wanted a dedicated relaxation area, and "to squeeze in as many double beds as possible, and I wanted them to be proper beds – that was important. I designed it on a scrap of paper, which I've since lost."

He retained a lot of the old signage, including "Mind Your Head" and, of course, the classic, relatively steep staircase. He even kept the old cigarette burns and titbits of etched graffiti, which he views as "the scars of life".

The design of the lower deck was dictated by practicalities and, principally, by three factors: the need to keep the added weight on the lower level, the even distribution of that weight, and what Adam could change and what couldn't be altered, such as the engine and wheel arches. As well as the original driver's cab and staircase, there's a boiler, bathroom, long open kitchen, wood-burning stove and two more rows of lengthways-facing seating. A removable dining table is sandwiched between the seats.

FUNCTIONALITY

Upstairs Adam created separate bedrooms by removing the original seats and building simple stud walls. Because the bus moves and has a life of its own, he felt it best that the walls should have a flexible finish, so rather than use a traditional plaster finish he used tongue-and-groove panelling. He investigated what insulation the bus came with, but on removing the inner skin he realised there wasn't any. He installed modern sheet insulation and then re-clad the interior surfaces with wooden panelling.

Figuring out where to place the kitchen was informed by the existing layout of the downstairs area. The driver's cab and entrance were at one end, and the natural width at the back

A ROOM WITH A VIEW
At the front of the upper deck (always the most prized position on any bus trip) he made use of the original seats to create a chill-out area with a great view from on high.

SLEEPING AREA
All the beds are on the upper deck, divided into their own neat rooms for extra privacy.

ORIGINAL FEATURES
Adam wanted to keep as many original features as possible to preserve the bus's character. When you're travelling on a bus the bells, seats and handrails don't usually catch your attention, but out of context you notice their design, their functional and sturdy manufacture, and their charm.

LESSONS LEARNT

Adam ran out of money halfway through the project and had to take time off to go back to the day job to replenish the coffers, but it was worth it – the finish is immaculate. And at the end, he took a trip back down to Cornwall to look at the land where his caravan was parked, but when he measured the access gate and space he realised that there was no way the bus was going to fit there. The solution came via some old friends, who had a rural property. They offered Adam a small wooded plot where he could keep the bus and run it as holiday accommodation. He has no experience of running a holiday business, but far from letting this deter him, he leapt straight in.

of the bus where there is bench seating across the whole area was kept as a sitting/dining area, although all the seating was re-upholstered and re-covered. Now, as Adam says, "It's a lot comfier than the normal back seat of a bus."

The natural place for the kitchen was opposite the bottom of the stairs. Adam opted to use off-the-shelf simple kitchen units because although he was a carpenter and could have made them himself, time was running out to do it from scratch.

THE STORY NOW

The bus is now parked in a semi-permanent fashion on a glamping site near Brighton. It has its own area in a wood on a farm and although it has not fulfilled Adam's original plan of being a surf-shack, it does have its own individual vibe as a rental holiday location. Running this has turned into a full-time job for Adam but it's worth it; this is a bus with its own spirit and character, and it's booked up for much of the year.

For Adam, this was a project on which he embarked with an incredible degree of self-belief, drive and ambition. Most of us would have shied away as the risk of it going horribly wrong was huge. His approach, which seemed to be a mixture of naivety, blind faith and sheer determination to make it happen, worked amazingly well, and this successful project has been, literally, a life-changer.

GEORGE'S TREEHOUSE

FOR ME, ONE OF THE MOST AMAZING THINGS ABOUT ANY CREATIVE PROJECT IS HOW IT ACTS AS A KIND OF FUEL. AS WELL AS GIVING ME GREAT SATISFACTION, I LEARN THINGS, DEVELOP MY IDEAS AND BENEFIT FROM WORKING IN A TEAM. IT STRETCHES ME AND INEVITABLY LEADS TO THE QUESTION: "WHAT'S NEXT?"

EVERY PROJECT I HAVE WITNESSED HAS TAUGHT ME DIFFERENT THINGS, OPENING MY EYES TO THE SKILLS, INSPIRATION AND EFFORT OF SO MANY TALENTED PEOPLE, AND BECAUSE OF THE SMALL-SCALE NATURE OF THESE PROJECTS, THINKING THE IMPOSSIBLE OFTEN BECAME THE OPPOSITE – THE POSSIBLE. THE TREE TENT WAS A CASE IN POINT: A SPHERICAL CANVAS STRUCTURE HANGING FROM ROPES BELOW THE TREE CANOPY. I LOVED THE SENSE OF ESCAPISM AND ADVENTURE AT BEING ABOVE THE GROUND – IT WAS A DIFFERENT WORLD UP THERE.

MY IMAGINATION WAS GALVANISED. I WANTED TO BUILD A TREEHOUSE AND TO TAKE THE CONCEPT OF BLURRING INDOOR AND OUTDOOR SPACES EVEN FURTHER, CREATING A SPACE THAT REALLY ENGAGES WITH THE LANDSCAPE AND EMBRACES THE CLEVEREST CUTTING-EDGE DESIGN WHILE CAPTURING THE MAGIC OF CAMPING. AND IT SEEMED RIGHT TO MAKE IT SOMEWHERE THAT EVERYONE CAN ENJOY, ESPECIALLY PEOPLE FOR WHOM THE JOYS OF CAMPING AND THE GREAT OUTDOORS ARE NOT USUALLY AVAILABLE; IT SHOULD BE ACCESSIBLE TO PEOPLE WITH DISABILITIES AS WELL AS THEIR FAMILIES.

"The freedom of being up in the trees is something I always envy."

STRUCTURAL LIMITATIONS

There was no doubt in my mind that my friend William Hardie, a talented master craftsman and designer, was the right person for this project. Apart from incredible workmanship, he brings remarkable conceptual elements to the design process. Our creative ramblings led to some wacky and wild ideas but although this process is key – and great fun – it has to work in tandem with practicalities. The location, for example, was challenging: a wooded site sloping steeply down to a small flood plain and a river with trees not structurally strong enough to support a treehouse.

We needed the technical expertise of a structural engineer. Our plan was to use sturdy oak posts, securely anchored to the ground, as supports. The posts would need cross-bracing with the vertical struts supporting the building; and the struts would occasionally be underwater as the site suffers from seasonal flooding.

This was no whimsical treehouse; it had to have serious design credibility as well as work with the topography, the climate and the accessibility requirements of people with disabilities.

CONNECTING STRUCTURE AND NATURE

Our objective was to create an accessible treehouse with separate spaces, or pods. We wanted to use rational, simple forms – the most basic shapes as building blocks – and then play with how to hold them up in the air. The more we could do to break down the boundaries between man and nature, the better. The location was within a national park, and the natural qualities of its environment provided our three key inspirations: water, trees and a vast sky with minimal light pollution. Each pod would relate individually to these elements.

RELAX AND PLAY

The triangular pod is part additional bedroom, part observatory – a place to daydream and chill out – a comfortable and flexible space. Roll-up camping futons, covered in traditional striped linen, big cushions and a box of vintage dominos create a suitably relaxed but fun environment.

A triangular A-frame would be the simplest of building shapes. Its two sloping sides would open to the vertical via hydraulics, to create an open roof and clear view of the sky. The interior would contain a simple sleeping platform.

A practical cube would be a modernist, sleek minimal building, visually connecting with the woodland by means of a deck and a large wall of windows opening directly onto the treetops, creating a curtain of green.

A cylindrical pod would provide a "wild camping" feel. Open-ended and looking straight up the course of the river, it would bring the light and sound, as well as the view, of the water into the space.

MATERIALS

Our choice of materials had to be sympathetic to the environment, aesthetically pleasing, practical, honest and capable of weathering. The triangle was the most engineered of the structures but the one that retained a rustic cabin feel and look. Using state-of-the-art steelwork and hydraulics in the most simple and pastoral of buildings is very appealing. The interior is plywood-lined and the large sloping sides of the building are clad in a traditional repeat pattern of cedar shingle, which will weather over time to a lovely silvery grey. Because of the stairs this is the only shape that isn't accessible by wheelchair.

Look carefully at the wall surface and the fine lines in the CNC-cut plywood indicate cut-out forms. Lift the pieces out and they slot together cleverly into stools and benches. The hidden surface exposed when the furniture is in use is a textural, rustic, cabin-style oak planking adapted from the engineered oak floorboards, lightly sand-blasted to expose the grain.

The cube is simplicity itself – a modernist box. The exterior is clad in blackened vertical planks of rough-sawn green oak, and here Will's inspired thinking and practical knowledge were instrumental in achieving an ingenious finish. He harnessed one of the natural properties of oak by brushing it with a solution of iron sulphate (tomato feed mixed with water); reacting with the natural tannins in the oak, the surface blackened within hours.

The cylindrical pod, by nature of its shape, had to be metal. A section of corrugated steel motorway drainage tube was the ideal solution. Ready-formed, its surface reflects the light and sound of the river and will oxidise over time. Left open-ended, it is a pure and raw form.

DESIGN FEATURES

I love the multi-functioning, clever design and space-saving devices that the designers of all past amazing spaces are so good at achieving. Squeezing the most out of every inch, without making a space feel cramped or haphazard, is a challenge. Here we tried to apply what we had learnt from those clever contributors and amp it up! Walk in to the cube pod and it looks like a minimal plywood-lined box, with bifold doors spanning the width and a deck running along the outside. There is very little detail.

However, along one wall is a simple cantilevered adjustable-height kitchen.

NORDIC COMFORT

The cube pod has a modern Nordic feel with echoes of Shaker practicality and aesthetics along with rustic cabin elements. The two modern Vitra chairs on the deck are a simple, elegant nod to the tradition of a rocking chair, together with a telescope for stargazing. The bed/sofa upholstery is a simple grey felt, the blankets a colourful graphic weave, and china, mugs and lanterns are white.

On the opposing wall, lines suggest openings, brackets hinge open and shelves fold down onto them to create a traditional Welsh dresser. There is a small gesture of a mantelpiece. Pull this out and the wall surface pulls down and out, too, becoming the dining table with small shelves in the wall behind.

The two single beds can be used as beds or a bed and a sofa. One folds down and swings out, separating the kitchen area and, in a simple reminder of its original form, small cut logs function as legs. The second bed folds down from the opposite wall and rests on two small swing-out cupboard doors. This is a really clever flexible space: you can pull out the pieces of furniture you want when you need them.

FINISHING TOUCHES

Jane, our stylist and co-author of this book, felt that the interior styling should reflect the character of each individual pod. She loved the architecture and design of the treehouse and believed that should lead the way. Each space needed a few carefully chosen additions to create an interior that was comfortable, beautiful, and as practical and stylish as the builds themselves. In their own way all the pods are clean-lined structures, which only need minimal furniture, so we selected small items that were in keeping with their design ethos and purpose.

The circular pod is an outdoorsy, semi-camping experience. It has a monastic feel with the small wood-burning stove and benches creating a contemplative and conversational space. A mixture of traditionally woven wool tartan blankets are piled up; if you want to sleep out, there are outdoor waterproof sleeping-bag covers and enough logs to keep the fire lit all night.

CREATING HAPPY MEMORIES

This entire project has been an amazing experience for me. The treehouses of my childhood were simple things: a few sticks, impromptu structures, more or less a shed in a tree. They were great times and gave my friends and me a lot of fun and enjoyment. It was fantastic to tap into that feeling again by creating something really special, not just for us but also to enable other people to experience great design, get outside and connect with the natural world. I wanted them to see in the details and beauty of this place just how good design can be.

"Up in the trees I was a child again."

BRAVING THE ELEMENTS
The circular pod is the one that brings you closest to nature in that it is permanently open to the elements. You can sleep there if you want to make the most of the setting – in which case there are rudimentary but invaluable outdoor camping accessories ready for use.

GLASTONBURY E-DENS

GLASTONBURY AND ITS FAMOUS TOR HAVE A POWERFUL EFFECT ON THIS PART OF THE COUNTRY, AND THE PEOPLE WHO LIVE AND VISIT HERE. JOSEPH OF ARIMATHEA, WHO BURIED CHRIST, IS REPUTED TO HAVE COME HERE, AND IT IS ALSO IDENTIFIED WITH THE HOLY GRAIL, KING ARTHUR AND THE LEGENDARY ISLE OF AVALON. ALL GOOD ARCHITECTS KNOW THAT IF A BUILDING IS TO BE SUCCESSFUL ITS LOCATION IS KEY, AND, MOREOVER, THE SPECIFICS OF ITS ASPECT AND HOW IT RELATES TO THE AVAILABLE LIGHT, SPACE AND OUTLOOK CAN DETERMINE WHETHER IT'S A GOOD SPACE TO BE IN OR NOT. THESE E-DENS ARE A UNIQUE EXAMPLE OF THIS, AT THE VERY FOOT OF GLASTONBURY TOR AND THE ANCIENT MYTHICAL OAK TREES NAMED GOG AND MAGOG.

THE PODS

As part of the renovation, expansion and development of their newly bought holiday accommodation, Jill wanted more accommodation to offer her customers. She turned to John Tucker, a local artisan carpenter, and he told her about some glamping cabins he was working on – beautifully designed, tear-drop shaped, single-room modern cabins, based on the principles of Fibonacci mathematics. Jill instantly fell in love with these aesthetically pleasing, well-proportioned pods. She felt that they were ecologically friendly and absolutely right for the place, and ordered two of them.

DESIGN AND PHILOSOPHY

John had developed the concept gradually over a period of time as he progressed from designing historically researched small spaces, starting with a replica Victorian bathing machine, to a shepherd's hut and, finally, to the E-den. At each stage he not only refined his design but also constantly evaluated what was right and not right with each build.

He wanted to design a pod that was simple and uncluttered both inside and out; was intuitive to use; had a pleasing shape; could be replicated; used sustainable and reusable materials; was a relatively large space to feel comfortable in; was made with zero-maintenance materials; and could be made easily in his own workshop and delivered to site on a simple trailer.

THE CREATORS

Jill Barker and her husband, Jonathan, settled in Glastonbury after selling their successful business in London. The incredible geography, history, legend and myths entwined with the place were not lost on them. She says: "There is definitely some truth in the legend – it draws so many different types of people here and they all seem to take away some sort of special experience. Sometimes I wake up really early and have to go for a walk up the Tor to watch the sunrise. Maybe that's magic or perhaps it's just me realising how lucky I am to live in this beautiful magical place."

Jill and Jonathan bought the holiday accommodation complex on impulse while checking out a potential school in the area for their son. Despite having absolutely no experience in the hospitality industry, the pull of the place was enough. They were looking for a new project and this was it. The cottages all needed renovation and the business itself was ripe for development.

John repeatedly sketched the shape, refining it until he felt it was perfect. Unsurprisingly, he discovered that the final pleasing curved shape had intrinsic meaning and a philosophy behind it. The Fibonacci spiral is mathematically correct, as well as aesthetically pleasing, and uses the golden ratio. John feels this goes hand-in-hand with good design, and although he hadn't started with this principle in mind, that was where he ended up! He produced a scale model of 1:12 to show to potential customers, so they could discuss how the concept could work for them and how it could be refined to meet their requirements.

MATERIALS

Based on a simple steel skeleton structure, the E-dens are of a sandwich construction. Plywood and MDF are sandwiched with 75mm (3in) "earthwool" insulation and a breathable membrane. The exterior is clad with locally sourced and milled larch wood, which is deliberately left untreated to weather over time to a subtle silvery grey. The wood is more or less straight from the tree, and no paint or stain is used on the exterior.

The roof is insulated with multi-foil (foam and foil layered material) and clad in steel. The awning isn't enclosed and uses strong, sturdy materials to meet John's requirements – scaffold steel poles and fittings – and all the parts are affordable and readily available. The canvas is heavyweight cotton.

A SENSE OF PLACE AND OCCASION

Here at Middlewick, Jill feels that the E-dens have been a fantastic addition to her business. Moved onto site ready-made on a low trailer, they were easy to place in the old apple orchard – their doorways and decks open up to views of the magical Tor.

The complex is used all year round, but when the festival is on at nearby Worthy Farm, it becomes home to the bands and musicians. They come with their friends and families, chill out, barbecue and make it their temporary home. Mumford & Sons, Dynamo and Carey Mulligan have all stayed here. Jill hopes that this magical place has inspired them all.

"The man who designed the pods has grown up surrounded by all the magical mysteries of this place, so it all fits together. And they're local and sustainable as well. Of course, they had to be set in the most stunning field with the best views of Glastonbury Tor in the old apple orchard under one of the ancient apple trees… and they had to be called Adam and Eve to finish off the story."

"Everything about the E-dens reflects the heart and soul of Glastonbury. Fibonacci mathematics, nature, the legend – they all have a purpose and a meaning." JILL

ENGAGING WITH THE OUTDOORS

The E-den reproduces the experience of sleeping out under the stars. As well as a Velux window to allow stargazing from the bed, the deck at the front and attached open-fronted awning create the idea of being at one with nature. The awning follows the line of the roof and the sides partially unzip and can be rolled back to create a more open-sided awning when required.

COSY COMFORT

Inside, a Velux window (with a black-out blind for when you don't want to wake up at dawn) is placed directly above the built-in double bed. The floor space beneath is left open, as are the wardrobe, shelving and work surface. There is one wide, stable-style doorway opening onto the deck.

LAMBRETTA TUK-TUK

WHEN DAVID ASKED HIS YOUNG SONS WHAT THEIR DREAM CAMPER VAN WOULD BE LIKE, THEY DESCRIBED THESE FEATURES: SOMEWHERE TO HANG OUT AND WATCH DVDS WITH FRIENDS; A LITTLE FRIDGE AND A LITTLE KITCHEN; CUP-HOLDERS; AND LOTS OF LITTLE WINDOWS WITH CURTAINS UP. SO, WITH A CAN-DO ATTITUDE AND A BACKGROUND IN DESIGN AND FURNITURE-MAKING, HE SET OUT TO CREATE A TINY PLACE TO HAVE FUN AND ESCAPE FROM EVERYDAY LIFE.

THE CREATOR
David Motely is a skilled designer whose trade includes making high-end furniture and bespoke leatherwork. He has a huge sense of fun and loves a challenge, qualities that make him a great dad to his young boys. Having restored quirky vehicles in the past, he was looking for a new project, and this time he wanted to go small...

FROM PICK-UP TRUCK TO TUK-TUK
Initially, David had been looking to convert a VW split-screen pick-up truck into a camper van. But his attention to detail and the relish with which he takes on challenging projects drove him to consider an absolutely tiny tuk-tuk-style Lambretta Lambro pick-up truck instead. Happily describing himself as "an absolute lunatic – a workaholic", he purchased the 1960 base vehicle from a scooter restoration shop where the owner was thinning out his collection. Lambretta had always made a three-wheel commercial vehicle as well as the regular scooter and this one was originally produced as a vehicle for Italian farmers.

David liked its curves, and the shape of the bodywork reminded him of Dougal from *The Magic Roundabout*. What's more, it was capable of taking half a tonne on its three little wheels. His plan was to use the front cab and the chassis from the base vehicle, but to replace the rear pick-up section with a more enclosed box structure. He was keen to preserve the characteristic shape of the vehicle, so the back had to match the curves of the front cab as much as possible, as well as needing to be of the right size and design for him to customise. The answer was fortuitously found in a box from another 1970s Lambretta Lambro commercial vehicle.

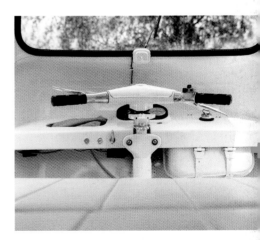

THE BIJOU KITCHEN

A tiny pull-out kitchen magically appears at the back of the camper van beneath the double opening doors. For this, David built a stainless-steel sub-frame and fixed it to the chassis. The kitchen sink, single cooker and small storage-jar section pull out in the style of a drawer and disappear when not in use.

LESSONS LEARNT

David is fortunate to be so skilled in so many fields, but just as importantly, he loves a chance to learn something new and he seeks perfection in everything he does, no matter how much time or patience it takes. He is principally self-taught and says: "If your mind is open, you can learn anything." And, when learning a new skill he adds, "I always buy the best equipment I can,; then I can't blame the tools." He could have opted for an easier build or more modest goals, but he viewed everything as a challenge and achieved a truly amazing space.

THE CONVERSION

Fortunately David has an engineering diploma, so he worked on the engine himself. Taking it all apart, he then installed an electronic ignition and a bigger carburettor and he increased the engine capacity.

He cut an opening in the back wall of the cab and an identical one in the rear box to allow access between the two. The box already had double opening doors at the back, but no windows. He even fitted a miniature kitchen facility at the back that could close away when not in use and leave absolutely no visible sign of its existence.

Knowing he wanted to fit some windows, he played around with the shape and number. He settled on three windows down each side, all square but with rounded corners and a relatively wide, laser-cut stainless-steel frame.

THE IMMACULATE INTERIOR

The interior looks clean and elegant, with a limited palette of colours and a neat finish. Exploiting his skills in leatherwork, David used two tones of leather in cashmere and cream to upholster the interior. The bed/seating in the back, the interior panels, the curtain hold-backs and the looped door pulls are all crafted from meticulously cut and stitched leather.

The windows have the same stainless-steel trim on the inside as the outside, and each has a pair of hand-made herringbone-weave curtains.

Amazingly, David's even managed to fit in two small storage cupboards that are made from painted MDF with rounded edges – and one of the cupboards contains a small fridge!

ALL IN THE DETAIL

The finish of the tuk-tuk is remarkable. David feels that if a job is worth doing, it is worth doing well. Notice the round wing mirrors. The original ones were the wrong shape and size for the driver to be able to see around the back of the van. David did his research and found circular mirrors from a truck in Wisconsin that are exactly the same size as the main headlight. He bent some steel tubing as arms for the mirrors. They look perfect.

Even the paintwork all over the gentle curves is beautifully done and, as David describes it, "It's vanilla – you want to lick it like an ice cream!"

GYPSY WAGON

MANY PEOPLE LONG FOR A SIMPLER LIFE IN WHICH THEY DON'T SPEND HOURS SITTING IN TRAFFIC JAMS OR DOING SOMETHING FOR A LIVING THAT THEY DON'T REALLY ENJOY. FOR KATUS, BARNEY AND THEIR YOUNG SON, MADDOG, THE SIMPLER LIFE HAS ALSO BECOME THEIR BUSINESS. THEY RUN A SMALL HOLIDAY COMPANY RENTING OUT HORSE-DRAWN WAGONS TO WORLD-WEARY CITY FOLK WHO WANT TO SPEND A FEW DAYS MEANDERING ALONG COUNTRY ROADS AND LANES.

THE CREATORS

When Barney Maurice was a little boy, his mother used to take him to visit a tinker who had a wagon that enthralled him. The smell, the nomadic life, the freedom – they all stayed with him. When he reached 16, he left home to work in a circus and stayed for over eight years, starting as a labourer and ending up as a manager. Some travelling followed, which led him eventually to the Isle of Arran, where he stayed to help set up a pony-trekking centre. This experience inspired him to buy a horse and an old traveller's wagon, which he fixed up; it was the start of a new career. Katus Young is a renowned world folk singer and songwriter who dreams of taking to the road, performing her songs and putting on a show along the way. They have a young son and three horses – all part of the family.

THE PLAN

Aside from running their own business and pursuing a musical career, Katus and Barney have a plan all of their own. They have taken their inspiration from a variety of sources, including a photograph of Barney's grandfather with a Brush wagon as well as the classic design features of Showman's, Reading and Burton wagons. The couple plan to live out their dream of taking a year out in France to hit the open road in a gypsy wagon pulled by horses and go touring. The wagon will even have its own stage, so Katus can perform her songs and invite local musicians to perform with her. As far as the music is concerned, it's going to be a "Horse Drawn Tour".

As they travel through France they will take another wagon with them, too, so paying customers can join them on their journey. This "horse-drawn hotel" will be an on-the-road version of their business at home.

THE DESIGN

Barney was so inspired that he felt he could create the perfect simple travelling wagon. Through studying photographs and books, together with his long-term interest and first-hand experience, he combined different style elements to create this unique wagon. He also added a door on one side to provide easy access to the stage, plus a mollycroft roof for extra height, light

and ventilation. While many of the principles of traditional wagons were incorporated within the design, Barney succeeded in creating a bespoke "square top" version that would suit their need for a living and performing space. They plan to install a solar panel in the wagon to power a small PA, some LED lights for the stage, and a laptop so that they can record their experiences via a daily blog for friends, family and other people to follow.

THE BUILD

The chassis (or the "underworks", as Barney quaintly calls it) was an original one, about 100 years old, which was purchased from a horse dealer and wagon-maker. It was in good condition and has been repainted and given a new set of tyres. A blacksmith fashioned a brand-new shaft to fix onto the front of the chassis, and Barney created a braking mechanism from an old woodworking vice that he bought in a car-boot sale.

Starting with the floor as the base, the wagon was built up one step at a time. The basic frame was made from pine, creating the "ribs", and then the roof was constructed. Barney has an interesting and unusual way of working: first of all, he figured out the construction in his head, then jointed all the pieces together accordingly. He built the wagon to get the shape he wanted, thinking about it as he went along, then dismantled and reconstructed it until he got it just right.

When the shape is correct, he sets to carving, which, apart from being a traditional form of decoration on these wagons

CARVINGS
The style of carving is symbolic in its subject matter; assisted by his friend Karim, Barney took "his own take on it" and they carved swallows on the back of the wagon as a reference to flight and freedom and their long journey south, which resembles the migration of the birds. On the front they carved horses to symbolise strength and power, and snails on the bottom as a nod to the idea of carrying your home on your back and slow travel.

and providing the visual signature of the creator, also serves the practical purpose of reducing unnecessary weight. This is a key requirement when horses are going to be pulling you along the roads. As part of the building and dismantling process Barney knows which pieces of wood are essential for the structure, and which ones can be safely removed.

THE INTERIOR

Inside the wagon is a traditional, highly decorative "Queenie" wood-burning stove which Barney plans to replace with a hand-made wood-burner, created from a recycled gas bottle for weight-reduction purposes, when they hit the open road.

Barney recognises that inside the wagon, it's better to adopt the handed-down wisdom of generations of travelling folk who have lived in such spaces and figured out what really works.

THE STAGE

Barney is still calculating how best to make a stage work for Katus's performances. His current aim is to use the base of a bow-top wagon as a separate stage area, which can be pulled alongside the main wagon so that it can serve as a backstage. The bow top of the wagon would be replaced when not in use, while the additional wagon would provide more accommodation.

TAKING CARE

To maintain the wagon in the best way, a fire should be lit to keep it warm and ventilated and it should be lived in and used, not left to moulder unloved in a garden. This wagon certainly has an exciting journey ahead of it.

THE BED

The main bed is at a raised mezzanine height in the traditional style, so it can be pulled out on an alternating wooden strut base to become a double bed when in use.

THE "MOLLYCROFT" ROOF

Mollycroft roofs have a raised central section, curved on top to follow the curve of the roof sections on either side. Being about 20cm (8in) higher than the rest of the roof and flanked by glazed, top-hanging casement windows, they provide additional light and extra standing space and improve air flow in the wagon, all of which makes the wagon feel more spacious.

LESSONS LEARNT

With Barney's uniquely organic method of construction, a lot of time is spent in quiet contemplation, staring at his work and waiting for inspiration to tell him how to carry out a certain task or overcome a challenge. He has to be patient and meticulous to endure the repeated creating, dismantling and rebuilding process, which is reminiscent of model making, albeit live and on a real scale. As he says, "I like to discover what I have overlooked."

THE BOXFISH CARAVAN

IT SHOULD COME AS NO SURPRISE THAT BARRY, THE
CREATOR OF THIS EXTRAORDINARY-LOOKING CARAVAN,
DESCRIBES HIMSELF AS A HAPPY-GO-LUCKY SOUL.
WHEN YOU HEAR THE CARAVAN DESCRIBED, IT SEEMS A
VERY STRANGE IDEA, BUT AS SOON AS YOU SEE IT WITH
YOUR OWN EYES IT MAKES YOU SMILE. ITS CHARM AND
HUMOUR WIN THE DAY.

THE CREATOR

Barry De Swardt, a native South African
living in the UK, works nine-to-five as
a landscape gardener. Both at work and
at leisure, his definition of a good day is
being able to create something new. He is
an optimist who likes to embrace life and
the opportunities it gives him. Practical
by nature, he trained as a carpenter and is
always ready to accept a challenge.

WHY THE BOXFISH?

One of the most amusing twists in this story is that Barry
absolutely hates caravans. He believes that their boxy design has
not evolved over the years and that "They have the aerodynamics
of a dead frog being towed by a snail." His original intention was
to take this on and to re-invent the caravan, but the cost would be
too high. Nevertheless, the concept stuck with him and he knew
that with some adjustment of his expectations, he could achieve a
lot within a much more modest budget.

So, why would anyone think of creating a caravan in the
shape of a fish – and why a boxfish? For Barry, it all started on a
deep-sea fishing holiday in Kenya. He did some snorkelling and
spotted a little blue-spotted yellow tropical fish. He chased this
amazing fish for almost a mile underwater. Later, he discovered
that it was a boxfish. The curious creature cropped up again in
an article he read on the plane home about a car manufacturer
that was designing a car based on the shape of a supremely
aerodynamic fish – the boxfish! The idea stuck and Barry started
pondering. He knew what he wanted to do; he knew what
materials he needed to use; he just had no clue as to how it would
all end up.

"What I've done is mad in a way, but only in a way that looks very yellow and spotty."
BARRY

DESIGN REQUIREMENTS

Barry knew that the traditional angular caravan was not for him. The teardrop shape was more appealing, but it had its own drawbacks: in his view, there was not enough space for normal everyday use, and it had no interior seating. So, he came up with something "teardrop-esque... a fatter, chubbier and uglier cousin of the teardrop. It is far more practical than a standard teardrop. Very aerodynamic and easier to tow."

The goal quickly became quite a test for Barry. "I just wanted to see if I could build something this mad in two weeks. The challenge was in doing it. So many people say, 'Aaahhh yes: I would like to build something like that one day,' and they never do. I just wanted to actually give it a go."

The majority of the design was thought out in Barry's head. He knew initially that this would, in essence, be a small caravan, so the internal space would need to be multi-functional: the seating should transform into a bed, there should be plenty of storage, both visible and hidden, there should be room for a kitchen, and gas and electric utilities should be fitted in. He decided to buy a secondhand two-berth traditional caravan, and the only crucial qualification should be that it have a sound chassis. The rest of it he would carefully cannibalise, keeping any materials or parts along the way that he could re-work into his new idea.

Trying to progress the shape of the design was difficult; he sketched it on the back of a restaurant menu, but it was a struggle to portray this organic shape accurately on paper. It would have to be led and informed by his step-by-step construction and the materials he used – as if he were making more of a sculpture.

A LITTLE LUXURY
The caravan interior isn't just a place to sit or sleep – there's room for luxuries, too. Barry's girlfriend loves to play music from their rockin' caravan, so he installed a £250 sound system.

THE BUILD
Barry had a self-imposed two-week schedule in which to complete the project. He had to be very practical and realistic. He wasn't going to waste time trying to save up pieces of old wood even though he was trying to keep costs down. He worked out early on what he could save money on and what he would need to buy new.

With the tight time frame, it would be hard for him to paint the exterior to mimic the yellow boxfish's characteristic markings, so he conceived of wrapping the caravan in a specially commissioned vinyl – a quick and effective solution. The frame of the caravan is made of plywood, fixed to a wooden base frame, and it was easy to bend it to form the contours of the fish shape.

THE INTERIOR

Inside the caravan, the key was functionality. Barry asked himself what he wanted from the space:

- A place to sit down and chill out in ugly weather
- A full-sized double bed
- Storage space
- To be able to listen to music and charge the phone
- A good fridge to keep beers and wine cold
- A proper kitchen would be awesome

He knew that the practicalities of the space would direct the style. His girlfriend, Dilek, would have some influence here and she chose the colour scheme and the materials – as well as the thumping music made possible by that luxury sound system! He's managed to fit in everything he'd longed for, and it's wonderful to see that such a unique-looking exterior contains such a cosy and functional inside. It certainly gets lots of admiring glances on the road!

RUSTY,
THE TIN TENT

AFTER RESTORING AND REDECORATING THEIR NEWLY
ACQUIRED FARMHOUSE SURROUNDED BY 12 ACRES OF
MEADOW, JON AND SALLY CONTINUED TO DEVELOP AND
RUN THEIR BUSINESSES AND BRING UP THEIR FAMILY. BUT
THEY STARTED TO WONDER HOW THEY COULD PUT THE
LAND TO GOOD USE INSTEAD OF JUST LOOKING AT IT.
IT WAS WHEN THEY ARRANGED A PARTY FOR OLD FRIENDS
FROM LONDON AS WELL AS NEWER LOCAL FRIENDS
THAT THEY CAME UP WITH A PLAN: TO LOCK UP THE
FARMHOUSE, ERECT A MARQUEE IN ONE OF THE FIELDS,
HIRE A BAND AND HAVE THEIR OWN MINI-FESTIVAL. THE
GUESTS WOULD ALL BRING TENTS OR CAMPER VANS AND
CAMP IN THE FIELDS, BUILD AN OUTDOOR FIRE, TALK, COOK
AND HANG OUT TOGETHER. SALLY DESCRIBES IT AS "ONE
OF THOSE MAGICAL MOMENTS: WE REALISED THAT WE
HAD THIS WONDERFUL LAND, AND EVERYONE JUST LOVED
BEING THERE. IT BLEW US AWAY HOW LOVELY IT WAS." IT
WAS TIME TO START ENJOYING THE LAND, SO INSTEAD OF
RENTING IT OUT, THEY DECIDED TO SET UP THEIR OWN
SMALL BUT VERY STYLISH GLAMPING VENTURE.

THE CREATORS

For Jon Taylor and Sally Biddle, a graphic and product design husband-and-wife team, a spark of inspiration struck when they left city life 12 years ago and relocated their business and family to a spectacular coastal farmhouse with 12 acres of meadows, formerly used for growing daffodils. It was a case of now or never – their chance to change their lifestyle and raise their young children in a cleaner, fresher and more outdoor and spacious environment. Jon himself had enjoyed an idyllic childhood growing up in the same area.

In an area of outstanding natural beauty with beautiful coastal views, this glamping unit blends into the landscape. The meadows are allowed to grow and paths are mown through the grass and around the edges. The small areas of woodland are managed and hammocks hang between some of the trees. The result is a happy combination of natural and man-made environments.

THE INSPIRATION FOR A TIN TENT

This enterprising couple started by doing their research and visiting existing tents before purchasing two canvas safari tents themselves. In their budget they included the additional cost of running in basic utilities from the nearby road; they already had a long-term plan to expand the number of units.

For their third unit they wanted something a bit different. They already used old shipping containers as additional storage for their business products, and their new idea was to create a totally unique glamping pod using a container as the base structure. The plan was to design and build a support for a large canvas tent-style roof, which would visually echo the look of the safari tents, as well as having a large overhang to provide shelter for a deck-style veranda at the front, and the kitchen and bathroom additions to the rear. And because the container would be more solid and sturdy than the tents, it could be rented out for longer in the season and even all year round, thereby extending the potential for growth within the business.

THE PLANNING

The site is designated as an area of outstanding natural beauty and the safari tents blend in with the landscape so well that they fell within the local planning authority's regulations. However, digging the trench for the utilities and getting permission from the local council for the container were inevitably going to involve meeting some stringent requirements. They sought professional advice and discovered they would require a comprehensive assessment of the land. So despite their project

A MUTED PALETTE

The textiles were selected to contrast with the hard materials and to add a touch of luxury to the stripped-back wood and metal. All the materials are in a grey/stone palette and are kept deliberately simple.

THE FLOOR PLAN

Jon sketched a plan, then refined it to scale with a graphics drawing programme. Step by step, the plan evolved: some of the elements from the two existing safari tents (e.g. the stoves and galvanised sheet-metal-style shower rooms) were kept, and new ones were added.

In this 12 x 3m (40ft x 9ft 6in) "Hi-Cube" container, there was enough headroom for a mezzanine-sleeping platform at one end with a double bed on the upper level and two single beds below. The main part of the container was set aside as a living area, with a dining table and benches, lounge seating and a wood-fired stove providing warmth and cooking facilities. A section at the front was removed to fit sliding double doors; a similar section on the rear wall was fitted with a door leading into the kitchen and bathroom, which were an additional extension. At the end of the container where the original doors are, a separate storage area was created, accessible only from the outside.

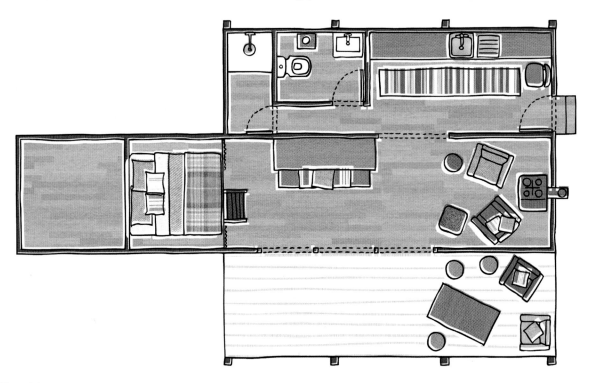

DECKING
To the front of the container, under the shelter of the canopy, is a large decked area with outdoor seating and a low coffee table made from a recycled pallet set on swivel wheels. Seats and side tables are made from tree stumps.

MODERN RUSTIC
The original container floor, which was part sheet wood and part metal and wore the scuffs and history of its commercial past, was sealed in its natural state. This was a deliberate decision in order to preserve the quintessential character of the container. Hence its life-worn finish was celebrated, and hardworking, natural, functional components and scraps were recycled or adapted to create furniture and materials.

being low-impact with a small footprint and in keeping with the landscape, they had to commission an environmental survey supplemented by an ecology and arboriculture assessment to keep the local and parish councils on board.

They had already set up "The Barefoot Kitchen", a glamping retailing website supporting local enterprises and celebrating the Cornish lifestyle, and this new venture developed that concept further. The local authority was keen to support and help grow local businesses and this was an important strand in their discussions. Another key part of the discussion was the huge natural legacy inherent in the land and local geography. They needed an assessment of the local wildlife, including bat and badger surveys, and when this was undertaken by the local authority, the land was found to be the site of a medieval settlement, so any digging would have to be monitored by an archaeological expert. This made the build more costly but, fortunately, the proposed site was well away from the badger sets, and the trenches dug for the utilities avoided any areas that were thought to contain the medieval settlement.

THE AESTHETIC AND MATERIALS

Sally and Jon have natural style, and they know what they like. They wanted to create something innovative, and the "tin tent" had to have integrity in its design and materials. Keen to avoid a clichéd "country style", they were inspired by the natural materials of the container and its place in the rural environment. Consequently, the direction they opted to take was a more industrial, textural, honest and rustic one, both in the materials and the decorative scheme. They liked the idea of it looking "sheddy" and "shacky". They were working to a tight budget, which worked both financially and aesthetically.

For example, the electrical trunking was left exposed; the mezzanine level was created out of welded steel; and OSB or particle board was used as a wall finish, as they liked its colour, texture and composition. The single beds were made out of scaffolding tube, as was the dining table; smaller-diameter tubing became the basic structure for the kitchen units; an outside tap was used as the kitchen tap; the pedestal stand for the washbasin is a chunky slice of a tree trunk and was left in its natural state with the bark attached; large wooden electrical cable reels were given new life as outdoor dining tables; railway sleepers set vertically in the ground act as windbreaks for the barbecues and fire pits; the roof of the kitchen, bathroom and shower room was made of translucent polycarbonate material to let in the light and through which the canvas roof's gentle creaking can be heard – one of the tiny but atmospheric experiences of camping. The pieces of container siding that were cut out to create doorways were re-used in the construction of the otherwise wood-built rear section – one as an external wall between the kitchen and the outdoors, and the other as an internal wall between the kitchen and bathroom; and roughly sawn, wavy-edged larch timber was used to clad the doors and exterior of the kitchen/bathroom annexe.

THE CANOPY

Measuring and putting up the canopy was stressful. As Sally says, "We really hoped those measurements were correct. It was the first project of this type that the marquee company had undertaken, and as such it was a prototype. To fit the canopy we needed a team of people, both on top of the container and on the ground. It took at least six men. It was incredibly heavy and unwieldy – up until then it had just been a container, but at that point it became a tent."

THE KITCHEN

The kitchen has a two-ring gas stove, which runs off a gas bottle beneath the work surface. Mains electricity powers a fridge, and you can boil a quick kettle of hot water or charge a phone by plugging it into the wall sockets. Saucepans and kitchen implements hang off a piece of metal conduit pipe and are suspended in a vertical row of small butchers'-style metal "S" hooks. The light fittings are simple dramatic metal-framed pieces, holding detailed filament bulbs. They came with names like "radio valve" and "squirrel cage", which say it all.

THE MEZZANINE

Steel beams were fitted across the width of the container, with scaffold planks placed between them as a sturdy base, and a surface of marine ply on top to create a smooth area around the double bed. A heavy metal stepladder was especially made to access the upper bed level. This had wooden treads attached and was safely secured to the floor.

THE CONSTRUCTION

Here, in an area of outstanding natural beauty, a single-track winding road leads down to a picturesque cove with its own beach. The container was ordered online from a local supplier and delivered by truck, but installing it wasn't easy. First it had to be craned over a 6ft hedge. The telegraph lines and poles follow the line of the hedge, so the container had to be carefully manoeuvred into place between the poles above the hedge and under the wires. Once over, it was lowered onto a flat-bed trailer and towed by a tractor across the muddy field. The crane was needed again to lift it off the trailer and onto the breezeblock base, and that, too, had to be towed by the tractor.

Using their friend Pete's metalwork skills, two doorways were cut into the container and reinforced with a metal frame. A timber extension was built onto the back using the remnants from the door cutting. The rest of the exterior was clad with wavy-edged larch and the interior with yacht-varnished marine plywood.

STYLING

Continuing the themes they had established for the materials and construction of the container, Sally and Jon chose a rustic, neutral palette inside. With their backgrounds in design, they knew instinctively what they wanted to achieve: an industrial aesthetic mixed with rustic elements, but, despite using some tough materials, it needed to be a warm, comfortable space.

Having all the hard-working materials around and on show can feel a little austere, and although they're rich in surface texture they don't always feel very comfortable and homely. To balance this, Sally has placed grey velvet cushions and plaid woollen blankets on the bed, along with naturally rumpled linen bed sheets. Reindeer-, goat- and cow-skin rugs, and more blankets and velvet cushions all enhance the space, making it feel more inviting. Mindful of the need for somewhere to hang an outdoor jacket, or a towel fresh back from the beach, Sally has fixed a number of galvanised hooks to the walls in appropriate places.

DESIGN OF THE CANOPY

Jon approached a marquee maker and between them they batted the issues and design features back and forth until they had the best solution. In particular, the methods used for tensioning the canopy needed to be figured out, and, as a design feature, Jon wanted a slightly curved rather than a straight edge between the guy ropes. The aim was to achieve a sculptural quality to the canopy and to use high-grade fittings to secure it.

A steel ridge line had to be built on top of the container on which the canopy would sit, and cross-struts would be welded along the container roof to keep it absolutely stable in the strong winds that blow in off the sea. The canopy was fashioned as a flysheet. Made of two pieces of NATO-green PVC-coated canvas, it was attached with stainless-steel plates, aluminium side poles, and tension straps with ratchet fittings. The design needed to be absolutely meticulous and specific, as did the maths. The securing wooden posts were fixed into the ground around the container and the detailed calculation and angles and measurements precisely worked out from there. There was only one go at getting this right.

FROM CONTAINER TO TENT

Sally and John are delighted with what they've created. Rusty, the tin tent, is open for bookings and they absolutely love it. As they say, "It's one of those rare moments when you have ended up with exactly what you had in your head – and that doesn't often happen!" Indeed, they like it so much that they stayed there themselves for a night with their children.

"We had a really lovely night. We cooked a slow-roast leg of lamb in the oven, and even though it was a stormy night it felt really cosy and lovely. It has such a tranquil feel and is a really relaxing place."

THE BATHROOM
Towel baskets are galvanised metal tubs, the wall storage an old wooden crate, and the shower walls ridged galvanised metal.

BERTIE BLUE, THE AMBULANCE CAMPER VAN

MENTION CAMPING HOLIDAYS AND YOUR AUDIENCE WILL DIVIDE INTO TWO OPPOSING CAMPS: THE ENTHUSIASTS WHO LOVE SLEEPING UNDER THE STARS, COOKING ON A LITTLE STOVE AND HANGING OUT WITH FRIENDS AND FAMILY; AND THE DOUBTERS FOR WHOM IT'S AN UNCOMFORTABLE, STRESSFUL EXPERIENCE. OFTEN THE SIDE ON WHICH YOU BELONG STEMS FROM CHILDHOOD MEMORIES OF CAMPING HOLIDAYS. DURING A PARTICULARLY WET AND WINDY BRITISH SUMMER A FEW YEARS AGO, JAY AND JONATHAN WENT ON TWO CAMPING HOLIDAYS WITH THEIR CHILDREN. THE WEATHER WAS SO BAD ON THEIR SECOND HOLIDAY THAT THE TENT POLES BROKE AND THE WHOLE FAMILY PACKED INTO THE CAR, GAVE UP AND WENT HOME. MOST PEOPLE WOULD BE PUT OFF CAMPING FOR LIFE IF THIS HAPPENED TO THEM, BUT JAY AND JONATHAN ARE MADE OF STERN STUFF, AND BOTH OF THEM HAD FOND MEMORIES AND A SENSE OF NOSTALGIA FOR THEIR CHILDHOOD CAMPING AND CAMPER-VAN HOLIDAYS. AND SO THE INSPIRATION FOR BERTIE BLUE WAS BORN.

THE CREATORS

When Jay was one year old, her family acquired a shabby old Volkswagen Bay Window Camper, which her older sister called the "Big Lorry". Three years later the battery fell through the rusted floor and the "Big Lorry" went to the even bigger car park in the sky. After that, her family embarked on a series of canal-boat holidays.

Jonathan's family also owned a camper van when he was a child. His father was a doctor, and when Romanian dictator Nicolae Ceaușescu was overthrown on Christmas Day 1989, Jonathan's father decided to drive the camper van – and his family – to Romania to deliver aid and medical supplies to remote villages and orphanages. Jonathan was an impressionable 12-year-old boy at the time. Today, Jay is a stay-at-home mum to their five children, and Jonathan is a primary school teacher. They have been together for 17 years, and have never taken time out to go travelling. "Our lives are based around the seven of us being together; that, to us, is the norm. It's how we work."

"I never claimed it was a good idea!" JAY

FAMILY OF SEVEN SEEKS ADVENTURES

Following their two disastrous camping trips, Jay and Jonathan were chastened but not beaten. They hadn't lost their adventurous spirit; it was a case of how to deal with unpredictable and disruptive weather to prevent it from spoiling their family holidays. They agreed that nurturing a sense of adventure and making enduring memories are what it's all about. The words "camper van" entered their conversations and they started talking about buying one. Jay got fired up and hit some online auction sites to do some research. She freely admits that she only "stopped on the pretty ones and ignored the dull ones. The whole point of a camper van is to go out and have an adventure." The choice came down to a decision between fun versus practical, and, of course, fun won out.

A pretty 1969 British Motor Company ambulance in good running order came up. It was for sale locally, so she went on her own to have a look at it. The exterior had already been restored, but although the interior had been stripped out, the original stretchers and medical equipment were still stuffed into the back and it was a mess. Her first reaction was to go straight home, but after talking to its tattooed owner for 30 minutes she knew she had to have it, and this was before she had even heard the engine running.

With Jonathan's backing, she bid and won the auction at £2,801. Thankfully, the old ambulance started up first time when they went to pick it up and they made it home in one piece.

ORIGINAL FEATURES
This is a classic vehicle with great character, and Jay and Jonathan were keen to preserve the chrome, almost-lidded headlights and the lines of coachwork trim along the sides.

THE REFURBISHMENT

The next step was to get an MOT certificate, but making it roadworthy meant a painful £1,000 worth of repairs. They employed local companies to do the repairs and work involved in converting the old ambulance into a camper van that would sleep all of them. The welding and metalwork were carried out by CWD welding, while Awesome, a company based in Cambridge, tackled the interior.

They found Rob Kitchen, a mechanic who works exclusively on classic cars, and he used his skills and expertise to get Bertie up and running well. The old ambulance, in the way of many an old caravan or camper van, was given a name and christened "Bertie Blue".

THE DESIGN

The aim was to restore the exterior and to retain its original features if possible. To achieve this, they worked closely with Awesome, which was refurbishing the interior. Their brief was simply "to match and blend it with the outside". Jay says that the Awesome folk were good listeners but had great ideas of their own as well. "They would ask me a question, skilfully and subtly pushing me in the right direction, then giving me the credit for it. The great thing is that they were always right."

The interior layout was designed by Jay, who drew the outline of the space on the kitchen floor in chalk and then nearly burst into tears when she discovered how small it was – only 9 x 6ft. And to compound the potential problem it's only 1.7m (5½ft) high and Jonathan is a lofty 1.93m (6ft 4in). After the chalk came the arranging of boxes and cushions to simulate the space. This worked better, but Jay knew it was time to get the squared paper and ruler out. She had no design experience but she was determined to get it right.

She had never thought of herself as a naturally creative person but this project helped her to realise that she had been harbouring hidden talents. She wasn't frightened to get out there and ask for help, and many hours were spent on camper-van forums asking questions. She was willing to roll up her sleeves to help but her biggest role was co-ordinating everything with the people that were doing the work, from the welders to the upholsterers to the mechanics.

THE KITCHEN
The simple kitchen area features two fitted side units and under-floor storage at the back of the van. The oak work surface on the right-hand side lifts up to reveal the sink and cooker beneath.

INGENIOUS MULTI-FUNCTIONALITY

A sliding, partially glazed door divides the driver's cab from the back of the van. The space can be reconfigured from "travelling" to "living" to "sleeping" mode. When travelling there are two front-facing and two back-facing seats in the main van, and two in the driver's cab (all with seat belts).

In daytime eating mode, the seats can be extended by pulling out a metal frame beneath them and adding a wooden base and additional cushions to create two rows of bench seating; the table also extends to a full width; this whole arrangement easily seats six (see pictures **1** and **2**, below).

In lounging mode, the seats transform into a U-shaped sofa.

In sleeping mode, the facing chairs pull out and extend to become two single beds (see picture **3**, opposite). Behind the window blinds are hidden roll-up hammocks. Simple cotton slings stretched between steel poles hook out from the walls and fix to steel vertical poles that extend from the chair backs (see picture **4**, opposite). The steel-welded frame in the chair backs and seats are welded to the chassis to provide sufficient anchorage and fixing points for the fibreglass ambulance structure. An additional middle section allows the two singles to join up into a large double bed (see pictures **5** and **6**, opposite). The two wooden kitchen units transform into a double bed at the back by a wooden slatted infill, and camping mattress (see pictures **7** and **8**, opposite).

And when friends and family come to join the family an additional Bell tent is pitched to provide extra accommodation.

Now fixed and fully fitted out, Jay and Jon love travelling in Bertie at his stately 18mph, although this means he is better suited to short journeys. They primarily use him for weekends away, finding places to stay and enjoying nature.

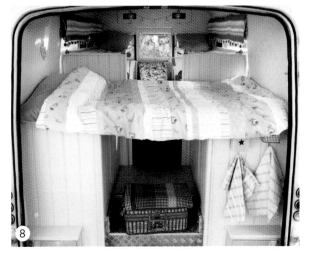

BEDROAM

THE BEDROAM IS A UNIQUE CONVERTED 1988
DOUBLE-DECKER COACH THAT DOUBLES AS A
COMFORTABLE MOBILE "HOTEL" AND A STORAGE
FACILITY FOR RACING MOTORBIKES. WITH ITS
OWN POWER, SLEEPING PODS, SHOWERING
AND TOILET FACILITIES AND LOUNGING AREAS
PLUS AN AWNING TO PROVIDE SHELTER FOR
COOKING AND EATING, IT IS A COMPLETELY
SELF-SUFFICIENT SPACE.

SOURCING A VEHICLE

Ollie started looking for a more comfortable and luxurious solution and found the 1988 coach on an online auction site. It had more character than a trailer or a lorry, so he followed his dream and bought it from some fellow bikers who had used it for transporting their bikes to events. The deciding factor was the vehicle registration document, which listed it as a private motorhome. So the coach ticked all the boxes: it had an historical association with bikes; it was mobile with a good functioning engine; and there was plenty of room to install two bathrooms and enough sleeping accommodation for his family and friends.

And outside of the motorbike-racing calendar the coach could be used for other events, such as overnight accommodation at a wedding, or as a changing and chill-out area for his girlfriend when she competes in adventure races with obstacles. The communal aspects of the project appealed to Ollie, too. He and his friends would all be hanging out together rather than in separate hotel rooms.

DESIGN AND BUDGET

Ollie's aim was to keep the cost of buying and converting the BedRoam below the purchase price of something similar. He's a practical man and he was confident that he could do a lot of the work himself by adapting and translating his competent industrial and agricultural skills. And by pooling their joint knowledge and specialist abilities, he and his friends had a good skill set for the work ahead.

Designing and configuring the space to best advantage was crucially important. The key factor was to maximise the accommodation and living space while still retaining a comfortable and luxurious feel. A lot of services needed to be fitted into the space: water, drainage, bathrooms, power. They had to be safe, well installed and hidden away with the furnishings and carpentry built around them.

Ollie thought a lot about this and struggled to find a designer or architect who would take on the challenge. Eventually he persuaded a local architect through a friend of a friend to do some rough sketches, and another friend who had worked on his family's farm and just finished a computer-aided design course did all the technical drawings to Ollie's specifications.

Inspired by high-end Formula One team coaches, Ollie's plan was to provide 18 luxury sleeping pods, each 1.5m (5ft) long, and two bathrooms on the upper deck, which measured 9m (29½ft) in length. The rows of pods could be placed lengthways along almost the entire length in bunk style, one above the other, and, with a 70cm (27½in) wide central corridor, every nook and cranny would be utilised. The two bathrooms would be positioned at the back and a new staircase fitted. The outside windows would be obscured by insulation and soundproofed cladding, and daylight would fill the space via the skylights along the centre of the coach ceiling, which would also provide additional headroom. Economical LED lights would be fitted.

The 16m² (172ft²) of downstairs space would contain four more pods as well as a lounging area. Outside a large awning would provide cover for further lounging, a kitchen and seating space for Ollie to work on his bikes. Hopefully, all this would create an atmosphere and environment reminiscent of a proper team bus!

As with many plans for unconventional spaces, this was modified over time – designing and refining the configuration of a space often go hand in hand. To make the upstairs more spacious 14 bunks were installed instead of the 18 that were planned originally, and downstairs the small seating area was altered to become more of a multi-functional space by the sofas folding up to become bunks in the evening.

THE WORK

The barns on Ollie's family farm gave him, his family and friends a large, sheltered and well-equipped space with access to power and utilities in which to store the coach, get materials delivered and carry out the work itself. This is a very important aspect of any project of this kind.

Although he planned to do the work himself, when Ollie stripped the outer metal side panels and glass off the coach, carefully saving them to replace at a later date, he quickly realised

SLEEPING ARRANGEMENTS

The sleeping pods themselves were assembled outside from 18mm (¾in) plywood with sound-deadening material installed at the back of each one. They were lifted on a forklift truck and slid into place through the open sides of the top deck, stacked on top of each other with the curved outer edge shape fashioned to exactly fit the shape of the coach interior. They all slotted well together – as George describes it, "like a horizontal game of Jenga!"

that a lot of structural work would be essential. In fact, the bus had to be completely gutted and much of the framework replaced and welded together. The outer panels, both metal and glass, needed to be restored to top-notch condition with a super-smooth surface for the final respraying of the coach and the sleek finish that Ollie was after. Any imperfections would be noticeable when resprayed.

Before the restored panels were replaced, the first fix of electrics was installed, along with water tanks and drainage. As soon as these were in place, the exterior was braced up.

A large proportion of the upper deck walls are composed of the glazed coach windows. The plan was to retain these, so the openings were kept the same size. When the glass was replaced, insulated and covered, it looked like "privacy glass" and the original exterior appearance of the coach was preserved. The front upstairs window was the only exception to this, being replaced with a piece of steel. Even the staircase was removed and replaced with a new structure. In fact, very little was left intact – this was a big project!

THE BATHROOMS

These are a feature of the coach that Ollie is particularly pleased with. They are unique. The space they had to fit into is very tight as it's at the back on the upper deck of the bus in a compound curve (curves in every direction). Ollie and his brother-in-law, James, mocked it up in plywood and then used "wet wall" to make the space watertight. The showers have timers that turn off the water, and the taps are equipped with sensors to control the amount of water used. Conserving water was a big issue, and although a 200-litre (53-gallon) water tank was installed, it needed to service a lot of people. Similarly with the lavatories, Ollie wanted something stylish and modern rather than the chemical type. They are air-powered, like the ones on planes and trains.

THE HARDEST THING

In projects like this one that don't follow a well-trodden path, a collective approach is always necessary, and for Ollie the hardest thing was finding the right people to do jobs in the way he wanted them done. He ended up working with friends who shared his passion for the project, like Warren the electrician and James the joiner. They were both involved in motorsport as keen fans or riders and they could see the potential in this project and believed in it. Although it was hard work, it was enjoyable and a welcome break from their everyday work.

Despite the day-to-day problems he encountered, Ollie never contemplated giving up. Sometimes, when he struggled to see an end to all the work, he would make a list of what he had to do and just take one day at a time. Focusing methodically on one job, one day after the next, kept him going.

MULTI-FUNCTIONAL SPACE
The downstairs space contains a lounging area with sofas – which convert to four further sleeping pods at night-time – and a fridge.

MISSION ACCOMPLISHED

It was the necessary recovery time from a bike accident that gave Ollie the impetus to start this project. His girlfriend wanted to go with him to races and bring their dog, so he needed to come up with a more grown-up plan. His dream was to build a hotel that could sleep 20 family and friends, his own team, when they came to watch him race, but it had to be mobile and provide space for his motorbikes.

"I was in hospital for a month after suffering a crash in a round of the British Super Moto Championship. I'd burst my duodenum when the bike landed on me, which resulted in a four-hour operation. Some biker friends who came to see me brought some caravanning magazines to take the mickey. This was my eureka moment."

LESSONS LEARNT

If means had allowed, Ollie would have bought a newer bus. Because it was 26 years old, a lot of worn parts needed to be replaced and it wasn't until he started peeling back the layers that he realised the full extent of the work that needed to be carried out.

"I'd always been interested in the amazing hospitality at motoring events and put two and two together and came up with the BedRoam."
OLLIE

You'd think a more modest project might do the job – something in between the rough-and-ready macho back of a van full of motor bikes and a luxury hotel coach inspired by the glamour and big budgets of Formula One, but Ollie wanted something completely different, which would outdo the tour-bus market and be customised for his own personal use. "I just wanted to turn up at an event, watch it, sleep comfortably, have a shower, then go... The dream gig would be the Isle of Man TT. I'd love to be parked up on the green by the pits with the bus. I used to want to race there but now I'm a bit older I'd be happy to just go with the BedRoam. I still want to be part of the scene."

TECH STUFF
This slick and stylish contemporary space isn't without technical wizardry. The satellite dish on the roof is a super-cool touch. Ollie has installed a big screen to enable his friends and family to watch sports while he's at an event. And there's built-in wi-fi, too. Guests will be able to link their computers to the screen, so if a team wants to show their telemetry, or even play a wedding video, there's the capability to do so.

INDEX

Page numbers in *italic* refer to the illustrations

ACKNOWLEDGEMENTS

FOR GEORGE

Amazing Spaces is a series that I'm incredibly proud of and it means so much to me and all the team involved in its production that everyone seems to love watching it as much as we enjoy making it. To make a television series that is not only inspirational to so many people, but also positive, friendly, warm and a lot of fun is a rare privilege indeed. I'm also lucky enough to be part of the some of the most exciting small-space projects you're ever likely to see; projects that simply put a smile on your face when you see them finished.

But there is no way the television series and this book would be a success without the hard work, care, thought and passion from so many fantastic people. In no particular order (as they are all amazing!) I'd like to thank everyone at Channel 4 for supporting the series every step of the way, in particular Jay Hunt, Gill Wilson and Kate Teckman and the great team behind them. A huge thank you to everyone at Plum Pictures for working ridiculously hard over the last year, with a special thanks to Will Daws, Jamie Wightman and all the production team. Thanks also to all crew, editors and photographers, particularly Chris Smith and Tim Pitot, who are collectively the unsung heroes of television for the amount of work they put in.

I'd also like to personally thank every single person who has built an *Amazing Spaces* project featured across all the series and in this book. You're a brave bunch! Thank you, too, to all at Quadrille for making another great book.

Very special thanks must go to two very special people. Firstly to Jane Field-Lewis, who not only helped write this beautiful book and style so many of the projects, but who also inspired the entire series. Without the lovely Jane none of this would have been possible. And to the very talented master craftsman, William Hardie (including Hamish and the rest of the William's team!) who help realise our great projects. Thank you.

And last but by no means least, I'd like to thank my children Georgie, Emilio and Iona who inspire me every single day. I dedicate this book to them.

FOR JANE

Amazing Spaces is a fabulous project and I find it inspiring and richly rewarding. My work as the creative consultant and stylist on the show means that I see first-hand the efforts, hard work and ambition of the contributors. I know that I speak for all of the team behind the show when I express our appreciation.

Channel 4, especially Jay Hunt and Kate Teckman, have had great confidence in this project from the start – when it was just a fledgling idea; to them I am very grateful.

I must also acknowledge Will Daws and Plum Pictures, who share the great effort needed to produce the show, and Jane O'Shea, Céline Hughes and Nikki Ellis at Quadrille who steered this book into reality. Above all, I'm grateful to the collaborative effort of them all, and to my ever tolerant family. These people enable me not only to produce some lovely work of which I'm proud, but they also make the work fun and allow me a genuine sense of achievement. I hope this comes across in the book and that everyone at home enjoys the stories behind the projects.

First published in 2014 by
Quadrille Publishing Ltd
Alhambra House
27–31 Charing Cross Road
London WC2H 0LS
www.quadrille.co.uk

10 9 8 7 6 5 4 3 2 1

British Library Cataloguing-in-Publication Data
A catalogue record for this book is available from the
British Library.

ISBN 978 184949 520 2

For Plum Pictures
Executive Producer Will Daws
Series Producer Jamie Wightman
Series Directors Angie Cox, Charlotte Whitaker and
 Anna Greenaway
Production Manager Stewart Batt
Channel 4 Commissioning Executive Kate Teckman

For Quadrille Publishing
Publishing Director Jane O'Shea
Creative Director Helen Lewis
Senior Editor Céline Hughes
Designer Nicola Ellis
Design Assistant Gemma Hogan
Photographers Ben Anders and Richard Maxted
Stylist Jane Field-Lewis
Illustrator Louise Begbie
Production Director Vincent Smith
Production Controller Stephen Lang

Printed and bound in Germany

Channel 4 is a trademark and is used under licence.

PICTURE CREDITS